JOURNEYS

Practice Book
Volume 2

Grade 3

HOUGHTON MIFFLIN HARCOURT
School Publishers

Contents

Words with *air*, *ear*, *are*

**Write a word from the box to complete each sentence.
Then read the complete sentence.**

airfare	hear	wear
airline	pear	year
dairy	share	
prepare	tear	

1. The _____ has ten airplanes.

2. Gently _____ the paper into two pieces.

3. The teacher will _____ the lesson for the day.

4. Did you _____ the bell ring?

5. You must pay the _____ before you can ride
   on the plane.

6. Milk and cheese are in the _____ food
   group.

7. You and I were born in the same _____.

8. It's cold outside, so you'll need to _____
   your coat.

9. This is a juicy _____!

10. It's kind to _____ your toys.

Adjectives That Tell What Kind

Adjectives are words that describe, or tell about, nouns. Some adjectives tell **what kind**.

We went for a <u>long</u> walk. (**What kind** of walk?)

An adjective usually comes before the noun it describes.

Thinking Question
Which word tells what kind?

Write the adjective that tells about the underlined noun.

1. We rode in a big <u>bus</u>. _____

2. It was a pretty <u>day</u> in the country. _____

3. We walked along a wide <u>path</u>. _____

4. Jason saw a brown <u>deer</u>. _____

5. A little <u>fawn</u> ran beside the deer. _____

6. A small <u>stream</u> crossed the path. _____

7. We had wet <u>shoes</u> after stepping into the water.
_____

8. The warm <u>sun</u> dried our shoes. _____

9. The path ended in a green <u>field</u>. _____

10. We saw lots of yellow <u>flowers</u>. _____

Name _____ Date _____

Lesson 16
PRACTICE BOOK

A Mr. Rubbish Mood
Introduce Comprehension:
Author's Purpose

Author's Purpose

Read the selection below.

Have you heard of the three *R*'s? They are reduce, recycle, and reuse. To reduce means to make less of something. You can reduce the amount of trash you throw away by doing a few simple things. Use both sides of a sheet of paper. Keep leftover food in containers instead of wrapping them in foil or plastic. Use batteries that you can recharge.

You can recycle many things, too. Remember to recycle your magazines and comic books. Recycle plastic milk jugs, metal soda cans, and glass bottles and jars.

The things you recycle are turned into new items. Recycled paper is used to make newspapers, cereal boxes, and wrapping paper. Glass you recycle gets turned into new glass jars and bottles.

Try to reuse things, too. Do you have a shirt that is too small? You can give it to someone younger. You can also cut it up and use it as a rag. There are many ways to reduce, recycle, and reuse items. Use the three *R*'s to help protect our planet.

Complete the Inference Map to show details in the selection that help you infer the author's theme. Write complete sentences.

Detail	**Detail**	**Detail**

Theme

Adjectives That Tell How Many

An **adjective** is a word that describes, or tells about, a noun. Some adjectives tell **how many**. An adjective that tells how many comes before the noun it describes.

She saw <u>three</u> birds in a nest. (**How many** birds?)

Thinking Question
Which word tells how many?

Write the adjective that tells about the underlined noun.

1. There are two <u>paths</u> along the river. _____

2. My dad hikes to the river with four <u>friends</u>.

   _____

3. Many <u>people</u> use these paths. _____

4. On some <u>days</u> the river floods. _____

5. Once the water rose six <u>feet</u>. _____

6. Water and mud covered several <u>fields</u>.

   _____

7. Five <u>days</u> later it was cleaned up. _____

8. The city set fifteen <u>benches</u> along the river.

   _____

9. I like to sit on a bench with a few <u>friends</u>.

   _____

10. Our walk home is about one <u>mile</u>. _____

Name _____ Date _____

Lesson 16
PRACTICE BOOK

Spelling Word Sort

A Mr. Rubbish Mood
Spelling:
Vowel + /r/ Sounds in *air* and *fear*

Write each Basic Word under the correct heading.

Vowel + /r/ Sound in *air* spelled *air*	Vowel + /r/ Sound in *fear* spelled *ear*
_____	_____
_____	_____
_____	_____
_____	_____

Vowel + /r/ Sound in *air* spelled *ear*	Vowel + /r/ Sound in *air* spelled *are*
_____	_____
_____	_____
_____	_____
_____	_____

Spelling Words

Basic
1. air
2. wear
3. chair
4. stairs
5. bare
6. bear
7. hair
8. care
9. pear
10. pair
11. share
12. near
13. ear
14. beard

Review
buy
year

Challenge
earring
compare

Review   Add one Review Word to your Word Sort. Which Review

Word cannot be added to the Word Sort? _____

Challenge   Add the Challenge Words to your Word Sort.

Name _____ Date _____

Lesson 16
PRACTICE BOOK

A Mr. Rubbish Mood
Writing:
Write to Persuade

Focus Trait: Ideas
Stating a Clear Purpose and Goal

A persuasive letter tries to make someone believe something or take an action. Good writers of persuasive letters state a clear goal. For example, Monique does not like the school lunch menu. She is writing to the people who make decisions about her school. Her goal is **to convince people that the school lunch menu should be changed to include more healthful foods, like fruits and vegetables.**

Read what each writer would like to see happen. Notice who the audience is. Choose the sentence that best expresses the writer's goal and would most likely be considered by the writer's audience.

1. I want to help rescued dogs and cats. My audience is readers of the local newspaper.

   A. Goal: Convince people to use a certain pet food.

   B. Goal: Convince people to adopt rescued animals.

2. I want our local park to be cleaned up. My audience is kids in my class.

   A. Goal: Convince classmates to volunteer to help clean up the park.

   B. Goal: Convince classmates to pick up after themselves.

3. I would like art and music classes in school. My audience is the readers of the local newspaper.

   A. Goal: Convince people that art and music classes are more fun than regular classes.

   B. Goal: Convince people that art and music classes can help students do better in other classes as well.

Cumulative Review

**Write a word from the box to complete each sentence in the story.
Then read the story.**

careful	energy	wear
center	shirt	worry
dirty	turned	
disappeared	stairs	

"I want to _____ my new clothes," said Julia. She went up
the _____ to her room and put them on.

Julia went back downstairs. She _____ the doorknob to
go outside.

"Julia," said Mom, "don't get your new clothes _____."

"Don't _____, Mom. I'll be _____!"

Julia _____ into the backyard. She used a lot of
_____ playing outside. As she came back in, she saw a big
spot in the _____ of her new _____. "Oh, no!"
she gasped. "I should have listened to Mom!"

Name _____   Date _____

Lesson 16
PRACTICE BOOK

A Mr. Rubbish Mood
Deepen Comprehension:
Author's Purpose

Author's Purpose

Read the selection below.

You break a wheel off your skateboard. You get take-out in plastic containers. What do you do next? You may throw these things in the trash. Think before you do!

Do you know what happens to an item after you throw it away? A garbage collector picks up your trash. The trash may get taken to a landfill. Most landfills are lined with a thick plastic or clay. Then trash is dumped on top. There are many problems with landfills. One problem is that we are running out of room! When a landfill is full, it is difficult to find land for a new one. Would you want to live next to a smelly landfill?

You may ask, "What about burning the trash?" If you burn the trash, you wouldn't need a lot of land for a dump. But once again, there are problems. Burning trash creates a lot of smoke and harmful chemicals. This leads to air pollution.

What is the best way to solve the trash problem? Recycle, reduce, and reuse in order to make less trash!

Use an Inference Map to determine the author's theme.
Then use it to help you answer the questions below.

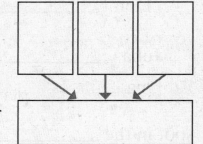

  1. Why did the author write this text?

_____

  2. What is the author's viewpoint about trash? Use
     details from the selection to support your answer.

_____

_____

Name _____ Date _____

This and *That*

1–5. Write the adjective that tells *which one* about the underlined noun.

1. What should I do with this <u>can</u>? _____

2. You could recycle that <u>paper</u>. _____

3. Please don't throw that <u>trash</u> on the sidewalk. _____

4. This <u>park</u> does not have very much litter in it. _____

5. Is that <u>bin</u> for plastic bottles or glass bottles? _____

**6–10. Underline the adjective that tells *which one*.
Then write the noun the adjective describes.**

6. My friends and I helped clean this park last week. _____

7. We put the trash we collected in that can. _____

8. This playground could use a good cleaning up. _____

9. Did you and your classmates clean that room? _____

10. I made this poster about recycling. _____

Name _____ Date _____

Word Towers

Read each clue. Write the Basic Word that matches each clue.

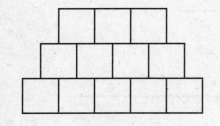

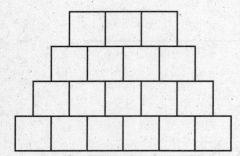

Clues

1. A body part you use to hear

2. Two of something

3. Hair on a man's chin

4. Fills the open space around you

5. A large, strong animal

6. Split something with a friend

7. Steps

Challenge Use Basic, Review, and Challenge Words to complete the Word Tower.

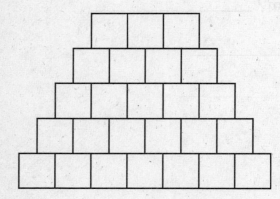

Clues

8. Pay money for something

9. Feel love and concern for someone

10. Furniture you can sit on

11. Steps

12. Tell how two things are alike

Spelling Words

Basic
1. air
2. wear
3. chair
4. stairs
5. bare
6. bear
7. hair
8. care
9. pear
10. pair
11. share
12. near
13. ear
14. beard

Review
buy
year

Challenge
earring
compare

Name _____ Date _____

Lesson 16
PRACTICE BOOK

A Mr. Rubbish Mood
Vocabulary Strategies:
Context Clues

Using Context Clues

Write the meaning of the underlined word as it is used
in each sentence. Circle the words that help you know
the meaning of the underlined word.

1. One weekend each fall, our family goes on a <u>yearly</u> campout.

_____

2. When it gets dark, we gather <u>kindling</u> to start a campfire.

_____

3. Last year, our tent was <u>leaky</u>. Rain dripped in while we were sleeping.

_____

4. This year we have a new tent. It is made from <u>recycled</u> materials.

_____

5. This year, we forgot to put our <u>garbage</u> in the trash can with a lid.

_____

6. A raccoon <u>gobbled</u> up the food we threw away.

_____

7. My brother and I <u>quarreled</u> with loud voices over who was supposed
to put the lid on the trash can.

_____

8. Pop got us to stop fighting when he <u>suggested</u> that we all go fishing.

_____

9. We got the <u>necessary</u> gear to catch fish and headed to the pond.

_____

10. We were sad to see the <u>pollution</u> in the pond.

_____

More Plural Nouns

- Form the **plural of a noun** that ends with a consonant and *y* by changing the *y* to *i* and adding *-es*.
- Identify nouns that change their spelling to form their plurals.

    The <u>families</u> enjoyed watching the <u>geese</u>.

1–5. Write the plural form of each singular noun in parentheses.

1. two beautiful (butterfly) _____

2. six new (hobby) _____

3. two intelligent (woman) _____

4. many falling (leaf) _____

5. a crowd of (child) _____

6–10. Write *singular* or *plural* for each underlined noun.

6. A <u>man</u> gathered bottles. _____

7. The <u>geese</u> flew over the recycling area. _____

8. Many <u>families</u> recycle their own garbage. _____

9. One <u>city</u> saves money by reusing paper. _____

10. <u>Mice</u> will eat garbage if it isn't cleaned up. _____

Proofreading for Spelling

Read the following journal entry. Find and circle the misspelled words.

Spelling Words

Basic
1. air
2. wear
3. chair
4. stairs
5. bare
6. bear
7. hair
8. care
9. pear
10. pair
11. share
12. near
13. ear
14. beard

May 8

    Today I went camping in a park nere my home. Before I left, I took cair as I decided what to where. I put on a jacket because the aer was crisp. I put a cap over my haire. I wore a pare of hiking boots, too.

    I got to the campsite and set up my tent. I sat in my camp chare and started to eat a juicy paire. All of a sudden I saw a big, brown bair. He was looking at my food, but I did not want to shear. I ended my camping trip right then and there!

Review
buy
year

Challenge
earring
compare

Write the misspelled words correctly on the lines below.

1. _____ 6. _____

2. _____ 7. _____

3. _____ 8. _____

4. _____ 9. _____

5. _____ 10. _____

Sentence Fluency

Short Sentences	Longer, Smoother Sentence
Our class watched films about the desert. We watched two films about the desert.	Our class watched two films about the desert.
There was a coyote in the film. The coyote was little.	There was a little coyote in the film.

Combine two short sentences by moving an adjective to make one longer sentence. Write the new sentence on the line.

1. The film was about a desert. The desert was beautiful.

_____

2. Many animals hunt during the night. It is cool at night.

_____

3. A fox had ears. The ears were enormous.

_____

4. The wind blows sand in the air. The sand is yellow.

_____

5. Few plants grow in the desert. It is dry in the desert.

_____

Words with /j/ and /s/

**Read each sentence. Choose the missing word
from the box. Write the word. Then reread the complete
sentence.**

season	decide	squirt
jelly	scale	jumping
force	edge	engine

1. Which _____ of the year is your favorite?

2. Close the door with _____ .

3. I used to want to drive a fire _____ .

4. Place the apples on the _____ .

5. Felice likes to put _____ on her toast.

6. The _____ on these scissors is too dull to

   cut cardboard.

7. "Did you _____ who is the winner?" the girl

   asked.

8. "If you _____ me, I'll splash water all over

   you," the boy warned.

9. We saw grasshoppers _____ into the

   bushes.

Articles: Using *a*, *an*, and *the*

- The words *a*, *an*, and *the* are special adjectives called **articles**.

- Use *a* and *an* before singular nouns. Use *a* before words that begin with a consonant. Use *an* before words that begin with a vowel.

- Use *the* for both singular and plural nouns.

    College students dug along (<u>the</u>, an) bank of a river.

    They were trying to find (a, <u>an</u>) old village.

    Long ago, Native Americans built (<u>a</u>, an) town there.

Thinking Question
Is the word after the article singular or plural, and does it begin with a vowel sound or a consonant sound?

Choose the article in parentheses that should be used with the underlined word. Write the article on the line after each sentence.

1. The students found (a, an) <u>arrowhead</u> made of stone. _____

2. They found some stones laid in (a, an) <u>circle</u>. _____

3. The stones showed where (a, an) <u>fire</u> had been. _____

4. One student found (the, a) <u>bones</u> of a dog. _____

5. (An, The) <u>student</u> held up the dog's skull. _____

6. Pieces from (a, an) <u>broken pot</u> were made of clay. _____

7. Strings marked off (a, an) <u>area</u> where the students worked.

    _____

8. They used (a, an) <u>little brush</u> to clean things. _____

Lesson 17
PRACTICE BOOK

**The Albertosaurus
Mystery**
Introduce Comprehension:
Conclusions

Conclusions

Read the passage.

Mary Anning was born into a poor family in England in 1799. Her father collected fossils for fun. He taught his wife and children about fossils. After he died, the family sold fossils to make a living. They found many fossil sea animals in the cliffs near their house.

Mary led the family in fossil hunting. She made valuable discoveries. She found the first plesiosaur, a dinosaur that lived in the sea. Scientists did not believe her at first because she was a poor woman. When they studied her fossils, however, they knew how important her discoveries were.

Mary became famous in her lifetime. People came from far away to see her. However, museums often showed her fossils without giving her credit.

Today, Mary Anning's story is well known. She has been called "the greatest fossilist the world ever knew."

On the Inference Map, write three clues and the conclusion.

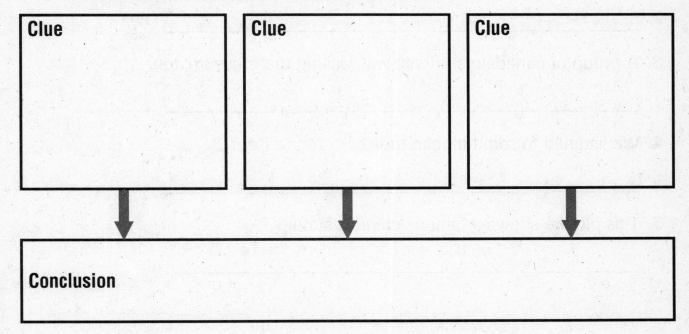

Clue	Clue	Clue

Conclusion

Capitalizing Adjectives

The Albertosaurus Mystery
Grammar:
Adjectives and Articles

- Some **adjectives** are formed from proper nouns.
- Adjectives that are formed from proper nouns always begin with a capital letter.

    We saw some <u>Mexican</u> paintings at the museum.

- The adjective *Mexican* is formed from the proper noun *Mexico*.

Thinking Question
Is the adjective formed from a proper noun?

Rewrite each sentence correctly. Begin adjectives that are formed from proper nouns with a capital letter.

1. I liked the egyptian statues I saw at the museum.

   _____

2. The japanese books were very old.

   _____

3. A group of canadian students was visiting the museum, too.

   _____

4. We listened to some african music.

   _____

5. This picture shows a famous chinese statue.

   _____

Spelling Words with /j/ and /s/

1. Write the Basic Words that use the letter *j* to spell the sound /j/.

_____, _____,

_____

2. Write the Basic Words that use the letter *g* to spell the sound /j/.

_____, _____,

_____, _____,

_____

3. Write the Basic Word that uses the letter *s* to spell the sound /s/.

_____

4. Write the Basic Words that use the letter *c* to spell the sound /s/.

_____, _____,

_____, _____,

_____, _____,

Challenge

1. gigantic Circle the letter in *gigantic* that makes one of this week's spelling sounds.

2. excited Circle the letter in *excited* that makes one of this week's spelling sounds.

Spelling Words

Basic
1. age
2. space
3. change
4. jawbone
5. jacket
6. giant
7. pencil
8. circle
9. once
10. large
11. dance
12. jeans
13. bounce
14. huge

Review
nice
place

Challenge
excited
gigantic

Focus Trait: Voice
Convincing Voice

Good writers of opinion paragraphs use a convincing voice. If you provide interesting details, your opinion will be stronger and more convincing. Compare these sentences:

Weak Voice: I think computers are stupid.

Convincing Voice: Computers can be a big help doing some tasks, but it's important to do more than just sit in front of a monitor all day. How about getting outside and playing with friends?

Read each sentence. Revise sentences with weak voice to be more convincing.

1. **Weak Voice:** Our cafeteria food is not very good.
   Convincing Voice: _____

   _____

   _____

2. **Weak Voice:** I think school sports are stupid.
   Convincing Voice: _____

   _____

   _____

3. **Weak Voice:** I think homework is boring.
   Convincing Voice: _____

   _____

   _____

Words with the VCCCV Pattern

Write a word from the box to complete each
sentence. Then read the complete sentence.

explore	partner	improve
instant	complaining	laundry
complex	dolphin	athlete

1. I know that if I practice I will _____.

2. We made _____ oatmeal since we had no
time to cook breakfast.

3. Cara is a great _____ who swims and plays
soccer.

4. When we paired up, I chose Gloria as my
_____.

5. Tran is always _____ that it is too cold.

6. This puzzle is too _____ for young children.

7. When we were at the beach, we saw a
_____ in the sea.

8. Mom is teaching me to do my own _____.

9. I would like to travel in space and _____ the
moon.

Name _____ Date _____

Lesson 17
PRACTICE BOOK

The Albertosaurus
Mystery
Deepen Comprehension:
Conclusions

Conclusions

Read the selection.

Frozen Dinosaurs

When you think of dinosaurs, do you think about hot places? Do you think about steamy forests and hot grasslands? Most scientists used to think that way, too. However, scientists have found dinosaur fossils in the coldest places on Earth, near the north and south poles.

The first polar dinosaurs were found in 1960. Scientists still have questions about these creatures. Did they live in the cold weather all year, or only for part of the year? How did dinosaurs survive in the cold? Was it as cold near the poles then as it is today?

Small and Speedy

Many of the dinosaurs found in cold climates were only two feet tall or smaller. They had large eyes, perhaps so they could see well during the long winter nights. They ate plants, and they ran fast on two feet. Some other polar dinosaurs were meat-eaters, though.

Searching for Clues

Scientists are searching for more clues about cold-weather dinosaurs. It is hard to dig for fossils in frozen places. But it is also hard to stop a scientist from wanting to know more. By looking at cold-weather dinosaur fossils, we may learn more about how dinosaurs lived.

On a separate sheet of paper, use an Inference Map to write details and a conclusion about the text. Then answer the question about making a generalization.

1. What generalization can you make about
dinosaurs?

_____

_____

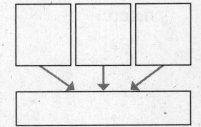

Name _____ Date _____

Lesson 17
PRACTICE BOOK

Comparing with Adjectives

The Albertosaurus Mystery
Grammar:
Adjectives and Articles

Choose the correct form of the adjective to complete each sentence. Write the sentence.

1. Were dinosaurs that ate plants (smaller, smallest) than those that ate meat?

   _____

   _____

2. Of all the dinosaurs, which one had the (longer, longest) neck?

   _____

   _____

3. I think that dinosaurs are the (greater, greatest) of all animals!

   _____

   _____

4. Some fossils are a lot (older, oldest) than others.

   _____

   _____

5. Was that dinosaur (taller, tallest) than I am?

   _____

   _____

Name _____ Date _____

Lesson 17
PRACTICE BOOK

The Albertosaurus
Mystery
Spelling:
Words with /j/ and /s/

Spelling Words with /j/ and /s/

1. Four of the words on the list are synonyms for *big*.
Write them on the lines. You may write Basic Words
and Challenge Words.

_____, _____,

_____, _____

2. Write three sentences about a dinosaur. Use
four of the spelling words. Don't use any synonyms
for *big*!

_____

_____

_____

_____

_____

Spelling Words

Basic
1. age
2. space
3. change
4. jawbone
5. jacket
6. giant
7. pencil
8. circle
9. once
10. large
11. dance
12. jeans
13. bounce
14. huge

Review
nice
place

Challenge
excited
gigantic

Name _____ Date _____

Lesson 17
PRACTICE BOOK

The Albertosaurus
Mystery
Vocabulary Strategies:
Suffix -ly

Suffix -ly

Circle the word in each sentence that has the suffix -ly.
On the line, write the meaning of the word.

1. The angry dog growled fiercely.

   _____

2. The truck driver honked the horn loudly when the light turned green.

   _____

3. Maria won the race easily because she is the fastest runner in our class.

   _____

4. We watched hopefully as Sean tried to score the winning goal.

   _____

5. When he saw his birthday present, Jason laughed happily.

   _____

6. The students read quietly in the library until the bell rang.

   _____

7. Mom told Sara that she sang beautifully in the school play.

   _____

8. We walked carefully across the shaky bridge.

   _____

Writing Proper Nouns

- A proper noun names a particular person, pet, place, holiday, or book title.
- Always begin a proper noun with a capital letter.
  Aunt Liz took me to the **Museum of Natural History**.

1–2. Identify the proper noun in each sentence. Then write each sentence correctly.

1. My favorite holiday is hanukkah.

_____

2. My friend tony and I really liked the movie.

_____

3–8. Use proofreading marks to write each proper noun in this letter correctly.

Dear grandma,

   Last week our class at beacon school learned about cats. We looked

at a book called all kinds of cats. My friend tracy brought her cat to class.

Her cat's name is fuzzy. Her cat was a valentine's day present.

                                        Love,
                                        Amy

Proofreading for Spelling

The Albertosaurus Mystery
Spelling:
Words with /j/ and /s/

Find the misspelled words and circle them.

A long, long time ago, a jiant ship flew through outer spase. It was the shape of a pensil, but it was gijantic. It flew in a sircle around the Earth. It flew around the Earth onse, then twice, then three times. In fact, it flew around the Earth a hundred times! What was it doing? What was it looking for? No one knows. Maybe the people on the ship wanted to chanje planets. Maybe they liked to bounse from world to world and never stop. Maybe their world was not larje enough for them. I have a different answer, though. I think they were looking for a place to buy geans. They just came here thousands of years too soon.

Spelling Words

1. age
2. space
3. change
4. jawbone
5. jacket
6. giant
7. pencil
8. circle
9. once
10. large
11. dance
12. jeans
13. bounce
14. huge

Review
nice
place

Challenge
excited
gigantic

Write the misspelled words correctly on the lines below.

1. _____   6. _____

2. _____   7. _____

3. _____   8. _____

4. _____   9. _____

5. _____   10. _____

Name _____ Date _____

Lesson 17
PRACTICE BOOK

The Albertosaurus
Mystery
Grammar:
Connect to Writing

Word Choice

Using exact adjectives helps the reader picture
what you are saying or writing about.

Less Exact Adjective	More Exact Adjective
a big bone	a gigantic bone
a pretty fossil	a beautiful fossil

**Replace each underlined adjective in the sentences with a more
exact adjective. Use the adjectives in the word box.**

purple	filthy	tin
fascinating	five	tiny

1. We read a <u>good</u> book today. _____

2. It was about a small group of <u>some</u> scientists in France.

   _____

3. This woman found <u>little</u> fossils in stones.

   _____

4. Some of the stones were <u>colored.</u> _____

5. The scientists put the stones in <u>metal</u> buckets.

   _____

6. At the end of the day, the scientists had <u>dirty</u> clothes.

   _____

Words with /k/ and /kw/

Read each sentence. Choose the missing word from
the box. Write the word. Then reread the complete sentence.

croaking	music	squeal
jacket	quiet	joke
squirrel	sock	tractor

1. Kim told a silly _____ that made us all giggle.

2. It is cold outside, so wear a warm _____.

3. After everyone went to bed, the house was very

   _____.

4. My brother's band plays rock and roll _____.

5. "Here is my shoe, but where is my _____?"
   Ana asked.

6. We saw a _____ in a tree at the park.

7. Mr. Martin got a new _____ for his farm.

8. The scared little pig let out a loud _____.

9. You can hear frogs _____ down by the
   pond.

The Special Verb *be*

> The special verb *be* has different forms. Different subjects use these different forms. *Am*, *is*, and *are* show present tense. *Was* and *were* show past tense.
>
> Ms. Greene <u>was</u> our teacher last year.
>
> We <u>were</u> interested in her book on deserts.
>
> One large desert <u>is</u> in Africa.

Thinking Questions
What is the subject of the sentence? Do I want to show present tense or past tense?

Choose the correct verb in ( ), and write it on the line.

1. Rain (is, are) rare in deserts. _____

2. A desert in Africa (is, are) almost the size of the United

   States. _____

3. Towns (is, are) far apart in the desert. _____

4. Some deserts (was, were) once grass-covered.

   _____

5. I (is, am) excited about the movie on deserts.

   _____

6. The movie on oceans (was, were) also great!

   _____

7. My favorite subject (is, are) science. _____

8. My favorite subjects last year (was, were) math and

   spelling. _____

30

Name _____ Date _____

Lesson 18
PRACTICE BOOK

A Tree Is Growing
Introduce Comprehension:
Text and Graphic Features

Text and Graphic Features

Read the passage and study the text and graphic features.
Then complete the Column Chart.

A Forest of Green Giants

The tallest forests in the world are in California. They are forests of big redwood trees. Many of the redwoods are taller than a thirty-story building!

The Hunt for the Tallest Trees

Michael Taylor and Chris Atkins hunt for tall trees as a hobby. For years, they have traveled through California measuring trees. In 2006, the two men found the three tallest trees ever measured.

Naming the Old Giants

The trees that Taylor and Atkins found are over *two thousand years old!* The men named one of the trees Helios, after the Greek god of the sun. They named the shortest one of the group Icarus after a boy in a Greek story. The boy flew too close to the sun. The father of Helios was named Hyperion. That is the name the tree hunters gave to the tallest tree in the world.

Tree	Height
Hyperion	379 feet
Helios	375 feet
Icarus	371 feet

Feature	Location	Purpose

Helping Verbs

Choose the correct helping verb in parentheses to go with each subject. Write the helping verb on the line.

1. Those workers _____ planting trees in the park. (is, are)

2. My brother _____ helping the workers. (is, are)

3. He _____ asked me to come with him. (has, have)

4. I _____ going to walk with my brother and the workers.

   (am, is)

5. Some trees _____ turning bright colors this month. (is, are)

6. One tree's leaves _____ turned brown already. (has, have)

7. Bugs _____ killed some of the trees. (has, have)

8. A park worker _____ spraying the trees to save them from

   the bugs. (am, is)

9. A bird _____ built a nest in that maple tree. (has, have)

10. Lightning _____ struck that big oak tree. (has, have)

11. I _____ hoping to see a tree like that. (was, were)

12. My brother _____ seen trees like that before. (has, have)

13. We _____ talking about trees and lightning yesterday.

    (was, were)

14. I _____ learned a lot about trees on my walk in the

    park. (has, have)

15. My friends _____ coming with me next week. (is, are)

Spelling the /k/ and /kw/ Sounds

Write each Basic Word where it belongs in the chart.

k̲ite	tr̲ick
_____	_____
_____	_____
	_____
c̲amp	**qu̲ack**
_____	_____
_____	_____
_____	_____
_____	_____
_____	_____

Challenge: Add the Challenge Words to your Word Sort.

Spelling Words

Basic
1. shark
2. check
3. queen
4. circus
5. flake
6. crack
7. second
8. squeeze
9. quart
10. squeak
11. quick
12. coldest
13. Africa
14. Mexico

Review
black
thank

Challenge
correct
question

Name _____ Date _____

Lesson 18
PRACTICE BOOK

A Tree Is Growing
Writing:
Write to Persuade

Focus Trait: Word Choice
Exact Words

Good writers of a persuasive problem-solution paragraph use exact words—nouns, adjectives, adverbs, and verbs—to express clearly what they want to say. Compare a sentence without exact words and a sentence with exact words.

Without Exact Words: The dog chased the cat.

With Exact words: The large, playful golden retriever chased the tiny calico cat.

Rewrite each sentence, adding exact words to express the writer's thoughts more clearly. Make up your own specific details and exact words.

1. The piano fell.

   _____

   _____

2. The puppy tripped.

   _____

3. The store manager told me to leave.

   _____

4. From the window, you can see many things.

   _____

   _____

5. The food was great.

   _____

Name _____ Date _____

Cumulative Review

Write a word from the box to complete each sentence about one family's love for the zoo. Then read the complete sentence.

complain	kiss	quality
exchange	monkey	question
instead	pick	surprise

1. I have never heard anyone _____ about our local zoo.

2. It isn't a huge zoo, but its _____ is very good.

3. Our zookeepers have managed to _____

animals with zoos in faraway places.

4. My favorite animal is a _____ from India.

5. He likes to blow you a _____ when you visit

his exhibit.

6. My little brother would _____ the zebra as

his favorite animal.

7. It's probably no _____ that my sister likes

the koala bears best.

8. Our family would choose a visit to the zoo _____

of almost any other form of entertainment.

9. We all often ask the _____, "Can we go to

the zoo this weekend?"

Text and Graphic Features

Read the selection and study the text and graphic features.

A River Giant

The Amazon River of South America is the largest river in the world. It is a little shorter than the Nile River, but it carries far more water to a much larger area of land than the Nile does.

Water for Millions

Hundreds of streams and smaller rivers are part of the Amazon River system. The river passes through six countries and provides water and a shipping route to almost half of South America!

Did You Know?		
• The Amazon flows 4,000 miles from Peru to the Atlantic Ocean.	• It pours nearly 400 billion gallons of water into the ocean each day.	• There are no bridges that cross the Amazon River.

Use a Column Chart with the headings Feature, Location, and Purpose to help you understand the text and graphic features. Then answer the questions.

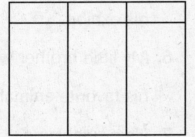

1. How is the information about bridges connected to the main idea of the article?

   _____

   _____

2. Based on the article and the text and graphic features, what conclusions can you draw about the Nile River?

   _____

   _____

Name _____ Date _____

Lesson 18
PRACTICE BOOK

A Tree Is Growing
Grammar:
Using the Verb *be* and
Helping Verbs

Using Verbs

1–5. Choose the correct verb in ( ), and write it on the line.

1. The pine tree (is, are) the tallest tree in the woods. _____

2. The lakes in our state (is, are) very pretty. _____

3. The Hudson River (is, am) the longest river in New York State.

_____

4. Our trip to Lake Erie (was, were) interesting. _____

5. We (was, were) happy viewing the lake. _____

6–10. Write *has* or *have* to complete each sentence correctly.

6. We _____ read books about the ocean.

7. Jack _____ written a report on rivers.

8. My friends _____ worked hard on their desert project.

9. The librarian _____ shown me books on mountains.

10. I _____ found pictures of tall mountains for my report.

Spelling the /k/ and /kw/ Sounds

Write the Basic Word that best replaces the underlined word or words in each sentence.

1. The recipe called for <u>four cups</u> of milk.
2. The mouse let out a <u>high, little sound</u> and then ran away.
3. The <u>little piece</u> of snow melted as soon as it touched my warm skin.
4. This is the <u>chilliest</u> winter day we have had this year.
5. Will you <u>look over</u> my report for spelling mistakes?
6. We have tickets to go to the <u>fun show in the big tent</u>!
7. With one <u>fast</u> kick, the player scored the winning goal.
8. When the king died, the <u>king's wife</u> became the country's leader.
9. Hold the egg carefully so that it won't <u>break open</u>.
10. My baby sister likes to grab my finger and <u>hold tightly</u> to it.

1. _____   6. _____
2. _____   7. _____
3. _____   8. _____
4. _____   9. _____
5. _____   10. _____

Spelling Words

Basic
1. shark
2. check
3. queen
4. circus
5. flake
6. crack
7. second
8. squeeze
9. quart
10. squeak
11. quick
12. coldest
13. Africa
14. Mexico

Review
black
thank

Challenge
correct
question

Challenge: On a separate sheet of paper, write a sentence using each Challenge Word. Then rewrite your sentences replacing each Challenge Word with a synonym. Use a dictionary or thesaurus if you need help.

Categorize and Classify

Some turtles live in the sea. Some turtles live on the land.
Other turtles are pets and live in houses. The words in the box below
relate to the different places where turtles live. Read the words.
Then classify, or sort, the words into the correct category.

tank	tides	soil	heat lamp	grass
waves	sand	water dish	ocean	box

Land

1. _____

2. _____

3. _____

Houses

4. _____

5. _____

6. _____

7. _____

Sea

8. _____

9. _____

10. _____

Subject-Verb Agreement

- Form verbs that show action happening in the present tense by adding -*s* or -*es* when the subject is singular and by not adding -*s* or -*es* when the subject is plural.

- Form verbs that show action happening in the present tense by changing *y* to *i* and adding -*es* when the subject is singular and by not doing so when the subject is plural.

A dog <u>runs</u> fast.	Three birds <u>fly</u>.
Horses <u>run</u> faster.	One bird <u>flies</u>.

1–4. Write the correct verb in parentheses to go with each underlined subject.

1. <u>Snakes</u> (move, moves) very quickly. _____

2. The <u>dolphin</u> (mix, mixes) speed and grace. _____

3. <u>Eagles</u> (search, searches) the ground below for prey. _____

4. An <u>owl</u> (cry, cries) loudly at night in the woods. _____

5–6. Underline the correct present-tense verb in parentheses. Then write each sentence correctly.

5. A cow (chew, chews) slower than most animals.

_____

6. A wet dog (dry, dries) slowly in the sun.

_____

Proofreading for Spelling

A Tree Is Growing
Spelling:
Spelling the /k/ and /kw/ Sounds

Find the misspelled words and circle them.

Dear Sam,

   I am having a great time in Mexico. On the seckond day of our trip, Dad took me snorkeling. I had to wear a wetsuit because the water here is the koldest I've ever felt! Before we got in the water, Dad called the beach patrol to ask a very important qwestion. He had to chek and make sure there was no sharck danger!

   Snorkeling was fun. We saw all kinds of fish. I even saw one called a clownfish. It was as colorful as a real circkus clown! Dad pointed out a fish trying to catch a little squid. We watched the squid scueeze out black ink. Then it made a quik getaway. It was amazing to see!

   Today my parents and I went to the market. We used some of the Spanish words we've learned. People smile and try to understand us even when we don't say things the korrect way. Sometimes we get the words all mixed up and just crac up laughing.

   We are having a lot of fun. I hope you are having fun back at home. I'll see you in a few days.

                                   Your friend,
                                   Mark

Spelling Words

1. shark
2. check
3. queen
4. circus
5. flake
6. crack
7. second
8. squeeze
9. quart
10. squeak
11. quick
12. coldest
13. Africa
14. Mexico

Review
black
thank

Challenge
correct
question

On a separate sheet of paper, write the misspelled words correctly.

Sentence Fluency

Short Sentences	Longer, Smoother Sentence
Mount Whitney is very high. White Mountain is very high.	Mount Whitney and White Mountain are very high.
Elise has hiked in the woods. Jamik has hiked in the woods.	Elise and Jamik have hiked in the woods.

Combine two short sentences by moving one subject to make one longer sentence with two subjects. Write the new sentence on the line. Be sure to change the forms of the verbs to match the subject of the new sentence.

1. A goat lives in the mountains. A wolf lives in the mountains.

_____

2. A hiker has stopped at the ranger station. A camper has stopped at the ranger station.

_____

3. My aunt likes hiking in the woods. My uncle likes hiking in the woods.

_____

4. Ellen has reached the top of the mountain. Steven has reached the top of the mountain.

_____

5. Ali was on the bridge. Jane was on the bridge.

_____

Name _____ Date _____

Vowel Sounds in *spoon* and *wood*

Read each sentence. Choose the missing word from the box.
Write the word. Then reread the complete sentence.

hooded	juicy	screws
sunroof	reduce	shouldn't
clueless	youth	rules

1. We asked the boy how to get to the mall, but he was _____ and couldn't help us.

2. To help the environment, we are trying to _____ the amount of trash we create.

3. We should use _____, not nails, to put the birdhouse together.

4. Our dog Rex likes to stick his head out the _____ when we take him for a ride.

5. My grandfather likes to tell stories about what life was like in his _____.

6. Before the game, the umpire reminded us to play by the _____.

7. You _____ run when the sidewalk is slippery.

8. Dad told me to wear my _____ jacket to keep my ears warm.

9. The _____ watermelon dripped on my shirt.

Irregular Verbs

The verbs **come**, **do**, **go**, **run**, and **see** have special spellings to show past tense. These verbs may also have other spellings when they are used with *has*, *had*, or *have*.

A mouse had <u>gone</u> into our house.

The mouse <u>ran</u> into the woods yesterday.

Thinking Questions
Is the verb in the past tense? Is the verb used with has, have, *or* had?

Write the correct past tense of the verb in ( ) to complete each sentence.

1. My sister had (went, gone) outside. _____

2. Tammy (saw, seen) the mouse in a pile of leaves. _____

3. My brother has (ran, run) outside, too. _____

4. Our neighbors had (saw, seen) the mouse on the bird feeder.

_____

5. The mice also (did, done) some damage to some feed bags.

_____

6. They have (ran, run) through the gardens. _____

7. The baby mice (go, went) into the nest. _____

8. I (did, done) a drawing of a mouse last night.

_____

Name _____ Date _____

Lesson 19
PRACTICE BOOK

Dogzilla
Introduce Comprehension:
Cause and Effect

Cause and Effect

Read the story below.

It was spring in Catville. Kittens played on the playground. Fluffy brought a ball of yarn for everyone to play with. Moms, dads, and children batted at the yarn. They pulled at the ball and chased the yarn. Soon Tiger came with another ball of yarn. Then Patches ran up with a third ball! The park was busy!

Suddenly, Mama Blinky cried out, "My baby! Where's my baby?" No one saw Blinky's kitten.

"Here, kitty, kitty," everyone called. Some cats looked under things. Some cats looked up high in the trees. The park became quiet as everyone looked.

Patches heard something. *Mew.* "Did you hear that?" Patches asked. He looked at the tangles of yarn dotting the park. *Mew.* Blinky ran to a large tangle of yarn. Her kitten was inside it! She pulled and bit at the yarn until she got her baby out.

"I have a name for you, little kitty," Blinky said. "Your name is Tangles from now on!"

Complete the T-map to show the cause and effect events in the story. Write complete sentences.

Cause	Effect

Irregular Verbs

The verbs **eat**, **give**, **grow**, **take**, and **write** have special spellings to show past tense. These verbs also have other spellings when they are used with *has*, *had*, or *have*.

> My mother <u>gave</u> me a chapter book about dogs.
> The author has <u>written</u> books about other animals.

Thinking Questions
Is the verb in the past tense? Is the verb used with has, have, *or* had?

Write the correct past tense of the verb in ( ) to complete each sentence.

1. I (wrote, written) my name on the cover of my book. _____

2. The first chapter (gave, given) facts about dogs. _____

3. I have (took, taken) the book to my friend's house. _____

4. She (gave, given) me a book about cats. _____

5. She had (wrote, written) her name in her book too. _____

6. Her dog had (ate, eaten) a corner of her book. _____

7. That dog has (grew, grown) a lot this year! _____

8. I (ate, eaten) a cookie before leaving. _____

Vowel Sounds in *spoon* and *wood*

Write each Basic Word under the correct heading.

Vowel Sounds in *spoon*	Vowel Sounds in *wood*
_____	_____
_____	_____
_____	_____
_____	_____
_____	_____
_____	_____
_____	_____
_____	_____
_____	_____
_____	_____
_____	_____
_____	_____

Challenge: Add the Challenge Words to your Word Sort.

Spelling Words

Basic
1. mood
2. wooden
3. drew
4. smooth
5. blue
6. balloon
7. true
8. crooked
9. chew
10. tooth
11. hooves
12. cool
13. food
14. pooch

Review
blew
foot
Challenge
loose
jewel

Focus Trait: Ideas
Thinking About Your Audience

Good writers ask, "What reasons will convince my audience to agree with me?"

Maia is writing to convince her parents to adopt a kitten. Her family lives in an apartment in a big city. Maia brainstormed reasons. Then she chose the one that her audience would care most about.

Cats get rid of pests, like mice, on farms.

Cats don't take up much room in an apartment.

Caring for a cat can be less expensive than other pets.

Read about each writer and his or her goal. Underline the reason that the writer's audience would care most about. Then add another reason that the audience would care about.

1. Rico is writing to convince his class to choose the zoo for a field trip.

   A. We can see the animals we've learned about in science class.

   B. The zoo has a special training program for adults who want to be zookeepers.

   Another reason: _____

2. Amber is writing to convince her dad to get a birdfeeder. Her family lives near a beach.

   A. In the mountains, birds cannot find food to eat during the winter.

   B. Many sea birds live at the shore during the winter.

   Another reason: _____

Cumulative Review

**Choose a word from the box to complete each sentence.
Write the word on the line. Then read the sentence.**

toothbrush	juice	food
shampoo	threw	shook
chewing	clues	
woof	lookout	

1. In comic strips, dogs often say "arf" or "_____."

2. To keep its owner safe, a guide dog is always on the

_____.

3. Some dogs use their noses to find _____ about the
right trail to follow.

4. Most grown dogs eat twice a day, but puppies need _____
four times a day until the age of three months.

5. Dogs should be washed with _____ made just for dogs.
Wash the dog all over, but try not to get the suds in the dog's eyes.

6. Sometimes a dog enjoys gnawing on a bone or _____ on
a special treat to keep its teeth healthy and strong.

Name _____ Date _____

Lesson 19
PRACTICE BOOK

Dogzilla
Deepen Comprehension:
Cause and Effect

Cause and Effect

Read the selection below.

Mice make good pets if they are cared for correctly.

Mice don't like to be alone. A group of female mice will get along well.
Male mice often fight. Three or four mice can live in a large glass aquarium
with a wire cover. They can escape a cage with bars. The bottom of the
aquarium should have wood shavings for the mice to make a bed in.

Mice usually sleep all day. They are resting for an active night.

Mice have sharp front teeth. Their teeth never stop growing. It is
important to keep a mouse's teeth healthy. It needs wood or chew toys to
gnaw on. Mice like to run in exercise wheels and climb little ladders. They
like to chew on and run through cardboard tubes.

A mouse can learn to sit in a person's hand or on a shoulder. It will eat
food out of a person's hand. Mice must be treated gently so they don't
get hurt.

**Complete the chart with your answers to the questions about
cause and effect.**

1. Why could a mouse get out of a cage with bars?
2. What happens to a mouse's teeth if it gnaws on wood?
3. Why do mice often play all night?

Cause		Effect
	→	Mouse escapes from cage.
Mouse gnaws on wood.		
		Mice play all night.

Irregular Verbs

1–5. Write the correct past-tense form of the verb in ( ) to complete each sentence.

1. The class (go, went) to the dog show downtown. _____

2. Some parents (come, came) with us last year. _____

3. The tails on some dogs have (grow, grown) very long. _____

4. One person (took, taken) her cat to the show. _____

5. We have (wrote, written) about the show for class. _____

6–10. Write the correct past-tense form of the verb in ( ) to complete the sentence.

6. Many dogs _____ tricks for the crowd. (do)

7. The dogs have _____ bits of meat as their rewards. (eat)

8. A friend _____ to my seat during the show. (come)

9. A Great Dane _____ the leash in its mouth. (take)

10. We have _____ some wonderful dogs this week. (see)

Vowel Sounds in *spoon* and *wood*

Use the Basic Words to complete the puzzle.

Spelling Words

Basic
1. mood
2. wooden
3. drew
4. smooth
5. blue
6. balloon
7. true
8. crooked
9. chew
10. tooth
11. hooves
12. cool
13. food
14. pooch

Review
blew
foot
Challenge
loose
jewel

Across
2. used to bite
3. to eat
7. not straight
8. what you eat
10. It is filled with air.

Down
1. small dog
4. made of boards
5. traced or sketched
6. opposite of warm
9. feeling

Name _____ Date _____

Lesson 19
PRACTICE BOOK

Dogzilla
Vocabulary Strategies:
Prefixes *pre-*, *re-*, *bi-*

Prefixes *pre-*, *re-*, *bi-*

**In each sentence, circle the word with the prefix
pre-, *re-*, or *bi-*. Then write the base word, the prefix,
and the word meaning.**

1. My mom can fix just about anything that goes wrong on a bicycle.

_____   _____   _____
    base word   **prefix**   **meaning**

2. I always go get popcorn during the previews at the movies.

_____   _____   _____
    base word   **prefix**   **meaning**

3. Jenna liked the book so much that she reread it three times.

_____   _____   _____
    base word   **prefix**   **meaning**

4. Hector and I meet biweekly to work on our social studies project.

_____   _____   _____
    base word   **prefix**   **meaning**

5. Our class visited a museum to see an exhibit of prehistoric art.

_____   _____   _____
    base word   **prefix**   **meaning**

Subject-Verb Agreement

- Add -s or -es to a verb in the present when the pronoun in the subject is *he*, *she*, or *it*.
- Do not add -s or -es to a verb in the present when the pronoun in the subject is *I*, *you*, *we*, or *they*.
- Change the *y* to *i* and add -es to form the present of verbs that end with *y* when the subject is *he*, *she*, or *it*.

  I **toss** my dog a ball.   I **fly** kites.

  She **splashes** into the lake.   She **flies** kites.

1–4. Write the correct verb in parentheses to go with each underlined subject.

1. <u>We</u> (train, trains) different dogs. _____

2. <u>We</u> (watch, watches) the dog do tricks. _____

3. <u>They</u> (perform, performs) great tricks. _____

4. <u>She</u> (study, studies) dog-training methods. _____

5–6. Combine each pair of sentences. Change the underlined words to pronouns. Write the new sentences on the lines.

5. Aunt Clara goes to dog shows. <u>Aunt Clara</u> loves all the different dogs.

_____

6. A cart carries small dogs to the ring. <u>A cart</u> brings them back, too.

_____

Name _____ Date _____

Proofreading for Spelling

Find and circle the misspelled words.

Dear Grandma,

Thank you for the wonderful day at the petting zoo. It put me in such a good moud. I remember hearing hooves as we walked across the wuden bridge. Seeing a mule up close was cule! I liked feeding it hay to chue.

It was fun to feed the animals handfuls of their special fuud. I liked petting the deer's smoath fur. I think the lamb smiled at me. It had a cute crooked tooth!

I really like the blue ballone you got me. It reminds me of our fun day. I droo a picture that I am sending to you. It shows you, me, the lamb, the mule, and the black pooch we saw. It is true that this day was the best one ever!

Love,

Quinn

Spelling Words

Basic
1. mood
2. wooden
3. drew
4. smooth
5. blue
6. balloon
7. true
8. crooked
9. chew
10. tooth
11. hooves
12. cool
13. food
14. pooch

Review
blew
foot
Challenge
loose
jewel

Write the misspelled words correctly on the lines below.

1. _____   5. _____

2. _____   6. _____

3. _____   7. _____

4. _____   8. _____

Name _____ Date _____

Lesson 19
PRACTICE BOOK

Dogzilla
Grammar:
Connect to Writing

Word Choice
Using Exact Verbs

Using exact verbs helps the reader picture what you are writing about.

Less Exact Verb	More Exact Verb
run	sprint, jog, dash, race
talk	whisper, chatter, gossip, debate

**For each verb, write a sentence that shows its exact meaning.
Use a dictionary if you need help.**

1. sprint

_____

_____

2. jog

_____

_____

3. dash

_____

_____

4. race

_____

_____

5. whisper

_____

_____

Compound Words

Write a word from the box to answer each clue. Then answer
the question below by reading the word in the shaded boxes.

chalkboard	flashlight	outside	toothpaste
cookbook	homework	snowshoes	underwater
fireplace	newspaper		

1.
2.
3.
4.
5.
6.
7.
8.
9.
10.

1. This helps you see in the dark.

2. You wear these to walk in snow.

3. You need this to brush your teeth.

4. Look here to see fish in a lake.

5. You do this work after school.

6. This is a book of recipes.

7. You might play here after school.

8. A fire in here will warm a room.

9. A teacher may write on this in a classroom.

10. You read this to learn the news.

What is the coldest place on Earth? _____

Contractions with *not*

You can put together two words and make a
contraction. An apostrophe (') takes the place of any
letter or letters that are left out. Many contractions
combine a verb with *not.* The contraction *won't* is
special. You form it from the words *will not* and
change the spelling.

*Ice-skating **is not** always a lot of fun.*
*Ice-skating **isn't** always a lot of fun.*

*The air **was not** very warm last night.*
*The air **wasn't** very warm last night.*

Thinking Questions
*Which verb am I
putting together with
the word* not? *Which
letter should I leave
out and replace with
an apostrophe?*

**Write the contraction for the words in parentheses. Use an
apostrophe in place of the underlined letter or letters.**

1. My skates _____ fit my feet very well. (do n<u>o</u>t)

2. Lamont _____ like the cold wind. (does n<u>o</u>t)

3. David _____ play in the snow. (will n<u>o</u>t)

4. My friends _____ skating most of the time. (were n<u>o</u>t)

5. Their coats _____ keep out the cold. (would n<u>o</u>t)

6. The town _____ put up a shed to keep us warm. (has n<u>o</u>t)

7. My parents _____ come to watch us skate. (can<u>no</u>t)

8. Your aunt _____ give us a ride home. (could n<u>o</u>t)

Main Ideas and Details

Read the selection. Then complete the Idea-Support Map.

Antarctica is the coldest place on Earth. You may think that there is no life there. However, some animals thrive in the icy seas and land.

Some of the largest animals on Earth live in the frozen waters of Antarctica, including orcas and humpback whales. The largest animal of all, the blue whale, also swims in these waters for part of the year.

More seals live in Antarctica than in the Arctic. Perhaps that is because there are few predators. Some of the seals that live here include the fur seal, the leopard seal, and the southern elephant seal.

You may already know that emperor penguins live at the South Pole. Many other kinds of penguins live there, too. Penguins are not the only birds at the South Pole. Majestic albatrosses live there, as do gulls and terns.

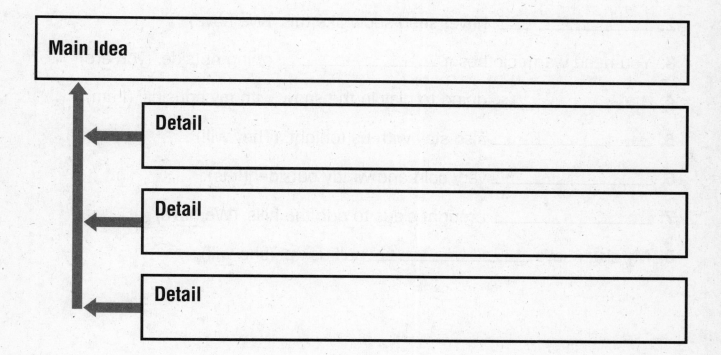

Main Idea

Detail

Detail

Detail

Contractions with Pronouns

You can put a pronoun and a verb together into one word to make a contraction. An apostrophe replaces the letter or letters that are left out.

*My aunt says that **she is** afraid of snow.*

*My aunt says that **she's** afraid of snow.*

We will *drive her home tomorrow.*

We'll *drive her home tomorrow.*

Thinking Question
When I join a pronoun with a verb, which letters should I leave out and replace with an apostrophe to make a contraction?

Write the contraction for the words in parentheses. Use an apostrophe in place of the underlined letter or letters.

1. _____ become too snowy to drive tonight. (It will)

2. _____ never seen snow like this. (We have)

3. You need warm clothes if _____ going outside. (you are)

4. _____ going to play in the snow with my cousins. (I am)

5. _____ also stay with us tonight. (They will)

6. _____ very cold and windy outside. (It is)

7. _____ brought sleds to ride the hills. (We have)

8. My sister says _____ pull us up. (she will)

Spelling Word Sort

Life on the Ice
Spelling:
Compound Words

Read each Basic Word. Listen to the number of syllables. Write each word under the correct heading.

Words with Two Syllables	Words with Three Syllables
_____	_____
_____	_____
_____	_____
_____	_____
_____	_____
_____	_____
_____	_____
_____	_____
_____	_____
_____	_____

Spelling Words

Basic
1. birthday
2. anyone
3. sometimes
4. everything
5. homework
6. afternoon
7. airplane
8. grandmother
9. something
10. without
11. himself
12. faraway
13. sunburned
14. daylight

Review
someone
cannot

Challenge
scorekeeper
everybody

Review: Add the Review Words to your Word Sort.

Challenge: Which Challenge Word has four syllables?

_____

Add the other Challenge Word to your Word Sort.

Focus Trait: Organization
Paragraphs for Reasons

Good writers make a separate paragraph for each reason in a persuasive essay.

Reasons Together	*Reasons in Paragraphs*
In Antarctica, scientists can learn about pollution. For example, they can find ash from Mount Vesuvius. They learn about how the climate is changing. They can see how quickly ice is melting.	In Antarctica, scientists can learn about pollution. For example, they can find ash from Mount Vesuvius. Additionally, they learn about how the climate is changing. They can see how quickly ice is melting.

Rewrite the following paragraph so that each reason has its own paragraph. Add connecting words between paragraphs.

A century ago, explorers built huts in Antarctica. Today, they are falling apart. We should save the huts because they are an important part of history. The huts are full of food and clothing. These items can teach us what the explorers' lives were like. The huts are full of books. By reading them, we can learn how explorers prepared for their trip.

_____

_____

_____

_____

_____

_____

Name _____ Date _____

Lesson 20
PRACTICE BOOK

Life on the Ice
Phonics:
Cumulative Review

Cumulative Review

Read each sentence. Choose two words from the Word Bank to form a compound word to complete each sentence. Then read the complete sentence.

bare	brush	eye	sun
bath	brow	fire	room
boat	butter	fly	sail
glasses	camp	foot	paint

1. When you do not have a shoe or sock on your foot, you

are _____.

2. You use _____ to protect your eyes.

3. To make a colorful picture, you use a _____.

4. The hair that grows just above your eye is called an

_____.

5. You take a shower in a room called a _____.

6. An insect that uses its pretty wings to fly from flower to

flower is called a _____.

7. A boat that uses wind and sails is called a

_____.

8. When you want to cook something while you are

camping, you build a _____.

Name _____ Date _____

Lesson 20
PRACTICE BOOK

Life on the Ice
Deepen Comprehension:
Main Ideas and Details

Main Ideas and Details

Read the selection below.

Who will be the first person to reach the North Pole? The question started a race to "the top of the world," and an American named Robert Peary wanted to win it.

To prepare, Peary traveled to Greenland. There he met Inuit tribes and studied their ways. He watched them build igloos, use dog sleds, and hunt. Peary learned about living and traveling in the harsh climate.

Peary did not reach the North Pole the first time he tried, in 1898. He set out again in 1905, making it farther north than anyone else ever had. Sadly, his dwindling supplies forced him to return.

In 1909, Peary, along with 23 other men, 133 dogs, and 19 sleds set out from northern Canada. Finally, on April 6, they reached the North Pole. Only six men remained in the expedition. Peary planted an American flag at the North Pole and turned homeward. Robert Peary and his team had won the race.

Answer the questions. Use an Idea-Support Map to organize your thoughts.

1. What is the main idea of this selection?

   _____

   _____

2. What details in Paragraph 2 support the main idea?

   _____

3. What details in Paragraph 3 support the main idea?

   _____

Contractions

1–5. Write the contraction for the words in parentheses. Use an apostrophe in place of the underlined letter or letters.

1. We _____ gone to the Winter Fair before. (have n<u>o</u>t)

2. My family _____ know how much fun it would be. (did n<u>o</u>t)

3. My sister _____ believe they had snow slides. (would n<u>o</u>t)

4. My brother _____ stop going down this slide. (can <u>no</u>t)

5. We _____ forget this fun day. (will n<u>o</u>t)

6–10. Write the contraction for the words in parentheses. Use an apostrophe in place of the underlined letter or letters.

6. _____ going to love the winter fair. (You <u>a</u>re)

7. Pat says _____ won a prize made of ice. (I <u>ha</u>ve)

8. _____ make a snowman for her contest. (She <u>wi</u>ll)

9. _____ melt if the sun comes out. (It <u>wi</u>ll)

10. _____ the best ice prize I ever won. (It <u>i</u>s)

Name _____ Date _____

Lesson 20
PRACTICE BOOK

Life on the Ice
Spelling:
Compound Words

Spelling Compound Words

Read each book title. Add a Basic Word to complete each title.

1. *Teacher, My Dog Ate My* _____!

2. *Using Sunblock to Avoid Getting* _____

3. *Happy* _____ *Rosalinda!*

4. *Sixteen Hours of* _____

5. *Traveling in an* _____

6. *Scott's* _____ *Pen Pal*

7. *Spending the Summer with* _____ *and Grandpa*

8. *An* _____ *at the Zoo*

9. *In the Rain* _____ *an Umbrella*

10. *Does* _____ *Know What Time It Is?*

Review: Choose a Review Word. Use it in a book title.

_____

Challenge: Choose a Challenge Word. Use it in a book title.

_____

Spelling Words

Basic
1. birthday
2. anyone
3. sometimes
4. everything
5. homework
6. afternoon
7. airplane
8. grandmother
9. something
10. without
11. himself
12. faraway
13. sunburned
14. daylight

Review
someone
cannot

Challenge
scorekeeper
everybody

Name _____ Date _____

Lesson 20
PRACTICE BOOK

Life on the Ice
Vocabulary Strategies:
Dictionary/Glossary

Dictionary/Glossary

Read each word. Write the base word to use to find its dictionary
entry. Then find each entry word in a dictionary or glossary.
Write all the ways the words can be used.

Word	Entry Word in Dictionary/ Glossary	Part(s) of Speech	Word with Endings
1. gliding			
2. hesitate			
3. dripping			
4. rippling			
5. horrifying			

Now write a sentence for one form of each word.

1. _____

_____

2. _____

_____

3. _____

_____

4. _____

_____

5. _____

_____

The Past Tense

- Form verbs in past tense by adding *-ed* or *-d*.
- Form verbs in past tense by changing a final *y* to *i* and adding *-ed* or doubling the consonant and adding *-ed*.

    The kids **piled** snow into a fort.

    Frieda **hopped** over the snow wall.

1–3. Write each sentence, using the correct past-tense form of the verb in parentheses.

1. The neighbors (hurry) to get their steps cleared.

_____

2. The snow finally (stop) after two hours.

_____

3. Parents (wrap) their children in warm clothes.

_____

4–8. Use proofreading marks to write verbs correctly.

Proofreading Marks
¶ Indent
∧ Add
⌿ Delete
≡ Capital letter
╱ Small letter

Dear Bennie,

   Yesterday a snowstorm movd into our area. We taged each other and

built a snow castle. We raiseed the walls higher. Later, the snow meltted.

My mother worryed that we would want snow every day!

                                                        Love,
                                                        Becky

68

Proofreading for Spelling

Read the following letter. Circle the misspelled words.

Dear Grandmoter,

    Thank you for my bithday card. It came in the mail this afternown. I love everthing you send me.

    I wish you didn't live in such a farawy place. Sumtimes I wish I had an airplan. I would fly to see you all the time. I could be back home when it was still daylite.

    Yesterday, I came home from school and played outside. I got sunberned. I canot play outside today. I have a lot of homwork to do.

    I can't say goodbye withowt saying I love you and I miss you. I hope you can come see us soon!

              Love,
              Tony

Spelling Words

Basic
1. birthday
2. anyone
3. sometimes
4. everything
5. homework
6. afternoon
7. airplane
8. grandmother
9. something
10. without
11. himself
12. faraway
13. sunburned
14. daylight

Review
someone
cannot

Challenge
scorekeeper
everybody

Write the misspelled words correctly on the lines below.

1. _____
2. _____
3. _____
4. _____
5. _____
6. _____

7. _____
8. _____
9. _____
10. _____
11. _____
12. _____

Conventions: Proofreading

Sentences Without Correct Contractions	Sentences with Correct Contractions
Shes bringing her sled.	She's bringing her sled.
The hill is'nt that high.	The hill isn't that high.
We have't walked up the hill yet.	We haven't walked up the hill yet.

Proofread the paragraphs. Find five mistakes in the spelling of contractions. Write the correct sentences on the lines below.

They're riding sleds down the hill. We cann't pass up this chance to sled. Ive never gone down this hill. You'have been here many times before.

It's a lot of fun flying down the hill. You should't try to stand up. Its not a good thing to do because you can fall. Everyone loves to go sledding on a cold day.

1. _____

2. _____

3. _____

4. _____

5. _____

Name _____ Date _____

Lesson 21
PRACTICE BOOK

Two Bad Ants
Phonics:
Base Words and -ed,-ing

Base Words and *-ed, -ing*

Read each sentence. Choose the missing word from the box.
Write the word. Then reread the complete sentence.

juggling	skipped	sliced
rattled	exciting	practiced
excused	tasting	unzipped

1. Travis _____ his jacket, took it off, and hung
it up.

2. The two girls _____ across the playground
instead of walking.

3. The clown is _____ four balls high into
the air.

4. The polite man _____ himself before he got
up from the table.

5. "It was _____ to see real giraffes at the zoo!"
Keisha said.

6. Did you cry when you _____ the onions?

7. When the snake _____ its tail, we took off
running.

8. I _____ my spelling words over and over.

9. The chef is _____ the stew to see if it needs
more salt.

Singular and Plural Possessive Nouns

- A **possessive noun** shows that a person or animal owns or has something.
- Add an apostrophe and *s* (*'s*) to a singular noun to make it a possessive noun.

  Dan found the <u>scientist's</u> report.

- Add an apostrophe to a plural noun that ends in *s* (*s'*) to make it a possessive noun.

  <u>*Ants'*</u> *homes are called colonies.*

Thinking Question
Which person or animal owns or has something?

Rewrite each sentence, adding correct punctuation for each singular or plural possessive noun.

1. We saw ants on Andreas kitchen floor.

_____

2. All the scientists books were about insects.

_____

3. Pats leftover food attracted ants.

_____

4. Kim discovered the ants homes.

_____

5. Many students reports were destroyed in a fire.

_____

6. An ants life has four stages.

_____

Name _____ Date _____

Lesson 21
PRACTICE BOOK

Two Bad Ants
Introduce Comprehension:
Story Structure

Story Structure

Read the selection below.

Ramon was the best fielder on the softball team. He just couldn't hit. One day, he bought a softball for a quarter at a garage sale. As he was walking home, the softball said, "Do you like to play ball? Are you any good?"

Ramon grabbed his bat and took the chatty ball into the backyard. He threw it up in the air and swung the bat, but he just couldn't hit the ball.

"You need help!" the ball observed. "Throw me up in the air and I'll move to the center of the bat. You just swing."

Ramon tried it, and he hit the ball to the corner of the fence. He tried again and again. Each time he hit the ball.

At Friday's game, when Ramon was up, he tossed the chatty ball to the pitcher. The pitcher threw the ball and Ramon swung hard. Crack! The ball sailed over the fence. Ramon had hit his first home run!

Complete the Story Map to show the story structure.

Characters	Setting

Plot

Problem (Conflict)

Events

Solution (Resolution)

Possessive Pronouns

1–5. Write the possessive pronoun in each sentence.

1. My class is learning about ants. _____

2. We watched a movie in our classroom about these insects. _____

3. Mrs. Greene brought to class an ant book from her home. _____

4. Do you know how ants find their food? _____

5. They smell the crumbs that drop from our sandwiches. _____

6–10. Use a possessive pronoun to take the place of the underlined word or words. Write each sentence.

6. Tanya and Rodney presented <u>Tanya's and Rodney's</u> ant projects to the class.

   _____

7. Lucy and Eric liked looking at <u>Tanya's</u> ant farm.

   _____

8. You must not let the ants escape from <u>the ants'</u> farm.

   _____

9. Rodney drew a picture of the ant in <u>Rodney's</u> jar.

   _____

10. The picture of the ant shows <u>the ant's</u> body and legs.

   _____

Spelling Word Sort

Write each Basic Word under the correct heading.

Words with *-ed*	Words with *-ing*
_____	_____
_____	_____
_____	_____
_____	_____
_____	_____
_____	_____
_____	_____
_____	_____

Review: Add the Review Words to your Word Sort.

Challenge: Add the Challenge Words to your Word Sort.

Spelling Words

Basic
1. coming
2. swimming
3. dropping
4. tapping
5. taping
6. invited
7. saving
8. stared
9. planned
10. changing
11. joking
12. loved
13. gripped
14. tasted

Review
making
stopped

Challenge
freezing
scared

Name _____   Date _____

Lesson 21
PRACTICE BOOK

Focus Trait: Ideas
Building Suspense

Two Bad Ants
Writing: Write to Express

Building suspense means keeping the reader guessing what is going to happen next. Here are some ways good writers do this.

1. Start with an event that captures the reader's attention.

2. Do not tell all the important details at once.

3. Use details to create an interesting setting.

4. Put a character on a deadline. If something doesn't happen by a certain time, a bad thing will happen.

Read the first description, with no suspense, and compare it with the second description, with suspense.

No suspense: The room was dark.

With suspense: He heard a fearsome Boom! Then, Crack! The howling wind and driving rain had knocked out the electricity. All Jose could see was blackness.

Read each sentence. Write new sentences to create suspense.

1. Natasha had to finish.

_____

_____

2. Alex wanted to show his father.

_____

_____

3. Mike heard footsteps.

_____

_____

Lesson 21
PRACTICE BOOK

Cumulative Review

Two Bad Ants
Phonics:
Cumulative Review

Read each sentence. Choose the missing word from the box.
Write the word. Then reread the complete sentence.

chopped	haircut	tripped
described	included	watermelon
driveway	racing	
driving	spinning	

1. The man admired his new short _____ in the mirror.

2. In the dark, Lee Ann _____ and fell over a chair.

3. Martin _____ the carrot into small pieces.

4. Mr. Edmond parked his big truck in the

   _____.

5. The cat is _____ in a circle chasing its tail!

6. A cap is _____ as part of your baseball uniform.

7. We ate juicy _____ at the school picnic.

8. Braden _____ every detail of the painting.

9. The two squirrels ran so fast they looked like they were

   _____ up the tree.

10. I saw an electric car _____ past our school.

Story Structure

Read the selection below.

Joshua stood on the riverbank. He cast his fishing line into the deep water. He closely watched the line for signs of movement. Nothing. He cast his fishing line again and calmly watched it.

"Come on!" Micah called. "This is boring! Let's go play up by Grandpa's cabin."

"You go on," Joshua answered. "I'm going to catch fish for dinner."

Micah shook her head as Joshua cast the fishing line again.

Two hours later, Micah walked back down the riverbank. "Are you still here?" she asked.

Joshua didn't answer. He just flicked his wrist and cast the line again.

"Mom is going to the store and wants us to go with her," Micah said. "I think she's going to get something to cook for dinner."

"Tell her we'll be having fish for dinner," Joshua replied and threw the line in again.

Answer questions about characters in the story. Use a Story Map to organize your thoughts. Then answer the questions.

1. How does Joshua feel about fishing?

_____

2. What problem does Micah have with fishing? What
story events support your answer?

_____

_____

3. How do you know Joshua is sure about his fishing skills?

_____

Possessive Pronouns

1–10. Choose the possessive pronoun in parentheses that correctly completes each sentence. Rewrite each sentence.

1. We have studied ants and other insects in (our, ours) class.

_____

2. Has (your, yours) ever studied insects?

_____

3. These insect books are for (my, mine) friends to read.

_____

4. The insect poster in the hall is (our, ours).

_____

5. (My, Mine) teacher suggested that we make the poster.

_____

6. Judy says that bees are (her, hers) favorite insects.

_____

7. Flies are a special interest of (my, mine).

_____

8. Janelle wrote about a talking wasp in (her, hers) poem.

_____

9. That old wasp nest on the table is (her, hers).

_____

10. (Their, Theirs) nests are interesting to look at.

_____

Name _____ Date _____

Lesson 21
PRACTICE BOOK

Two Bad Ants
Spelling:
Words with -ed and -ing

Words with *-ed* and *-ing*

Write the Basic Word that replaces the underlined word or words in each book title.

1. <u>Kidding</u> and Laughing _____

2. <u>Moving</u> to California _____

3. Stop <u>Letting Go of</u> the Ball _____

4. <u>Sticking Together</u> and Gluing Projects

   _____

5. <u>Moving in Water</u> Sports _____

6. <u>Asked</u> to the Party _____

7. Pets I Have <u>Liked a Lot</u> _____

8. <u>Keeping</u> Money in a Bank _____

9. We <u>Arranged</u> a Party _____

10. <u>Making Different</u> Weather _____

11. He <u>Held</u> a Baseball Bat _____

12. A <u>Hitting Lightly</u> at the Door _____

13. Teas I Have <u>Tried</u> _____

14. The Monster <u>Looked</u> at Me! _____

Review What Review Word completes this title?

The Art of _____ Bread

Challenge Write your own title using one of the Challenge Words.

_____

Spelling Words

Basic
1. coming
2. swimming
3. dropping
4. tapping
5. taping
6. invited
7. saving
8. stared
9. planned
10. changing
11. joking
12. loved
13. gripped
14. tasted

Review
making
stopped

Challenge
freezing
scared

Name _____ Date _____

Base Words and Prefix *non-*

Read each question. Add the prefix *non-* to the underlined word and write a new word. Use the new word to write an answer to each question.

1. What is your favorite book that isn't <u>fiction</u>?

_____

2. What foods without <u>fat</u> do you like best?

_____

3. If you could play a game for hours and not <u>stop</u>, what would it be?

_____

4. Is a smile a <u>verbal</u> way to send a message?

_____

5. When are you not very <u>productive</u>?

_____

6. You should never show anger <u>violently</u>. So, how can you show anger?

_____

7. Does the tongue twister "rubber baby buggy bumpers" make <u>sense</u>?

_____

Kinds of Adjectives

> Words that describe, or tell about, nouns are called **adjectives**. Adjectives can tell **what kind** or **how many** about a noun.
>
> Jasmine loves **sweet** foods.

1–5. Write the adjective that tells *what kind* or *how many* about the underlined noun.

1. Tara made chocolate <u>cake</u>. _____

2. Our diet has little <u>sugar</u>. _____

3. We eat three <u>kinds</u> of vegetables. _____

4. We drink many <u>glasses</u> of water daily. _____

5. My mother makes healthful <u>meals</u>. _____

6–8. Combine each pair of sentences. In the new sentence, use two adjectives to describe the same noun.

6. The vegetables are healthful. The vegetables are delicious.

_____

7. The pie was sweet. It was also juicy.

_____

8. The drink was thick. It was icy, too.

_____

Proofreading for Spelling

Two Bad Ants
Spelling:
Words with *-ed* and *-ing*

Read the following invitation. Find and circle the misspelled words.

Spelling Words

1. coming
2. swimming
3. dropping
4. tapping
5. taping
6. invited
7. saving
8. stared
9. planned
10. changing
11. joking
12. loved
13. gripped
14. tasted

Review
making
stopped

Challenge
freezing
scared

You Are Invited To A Swiming Party!

Parents will be droping kids at the planed meeting place: the changging rooms at Bayview Park. Everyone is coming at 11:00.

I have been saveing plastic flowers. We will be tapeing them onto our bathing caps. People stared when we did this at my sister's party. I think they all lovved how we looked and knew we were only jokeing.

We will play in the water until noon. We griped hands at my sister's party and jumped over waves. Maybe we can do that again! Then my dad will make a tapping signal. He will serve chicken and salad for lunch. I've tastted his cooking and it will be great! Finally, we'll have a second swim. It will be a fun party. I hope you can make it!

Write the misspelled words correctly on the lines below.

1. _____   6. _____
2. _____   7. _____
3. _____   8. _____
4. _____   9. _____
5. _____   10. _____

Name _____ Date _____

Ideas

You can make a sentence clearer by adding a possessive noun or pronoun that tells more about the subject. Put the noun or pronoun and any words that go with it right after the subject. Use a comma (,) before and after the words you add about the subject. Use an apostrophe with the possessive noun.

Less Clear	Clearer
Harry is looking for ants to study.	Harry, Susan's friend, is looking for ants to study.
Martha likes learning about insects.	Martha, his big sister, likes learning about insects.

Add the possessive nouns or pronouns in parentheses to each underlined noun. Write the new sentence with commas before and after the words you add.

1. <u>Raul</u> went on the field trip, too. (Carmen's brother)

   _____

2. <u>Greg</u> went back out with the group. (Oscar's dad)

   _____

3. <u>Donna</u> stayed at home. (Raul's mother)

   _____

4. <u>Jenna</u> was the first to find an ant colony. (his science partner)

   _____

5. <u>Jeff</u> found the class by the lake. (our buddy)

   _____

Lesson 22
PRACTICE BOOK

**The Journey:
Stories of Migration**
Phonics: Spelling Changes:
-s, -es, -ed, -ing

Spelling Changes:
-s, -es, -ed, -ing

**Read each sentence. Choose the missing word from the box.
Write the word. Then reread the complete sentence.**

hurried	drying	cities
replied	pennies	grazed
traveled	memories	
pillows	paintbrushes	

1. April _____ to the question with another
question.

2. I have such good _____ of my first day in
kindergarten.

3. Most of the big _____ in California are on
the coast.

4. The goats _____ on the hillside.

5. Ten _____ equal one dime.

6. Alexander _____ to school so he wouldn't
be late.

7. The class _____ to the zoo on a bus.

8. Joshua broke a plate as he was _____ the
dishes.

9. Mom set two fluffy _____ on the bed.

10. I need several _____ to paint the wall.

Names for Days, Months, and Holidays

There are many kinds of **proper nouns**. Always begin a proper noun with a capital letter. Begin names of days, months, and holidays with a capital letter.

We drove 150 miles on **Memorial Day**.

From **January** to **March**, the birds flew more than 1,000 miles.

Thinking Question
Is the word the name of a particular day, month, or holiday?

Write each sentence correctly. Capitalize the names of particular days, months, holidays, or special events.

1. His map showed that the birds would migrate in april.

_____

2. We traveled from presidents' day until valentine's day.

_____

3. I think mother's day is on sunday, may 13.

_____

4. We finished our project about birds on friday.

_____

5. The family attended the thanksgiving dinner.

_____

Name _____ Date _____

Lesson 22
PRACTICE BOOK

The Journey:
Stories of Migration
Introduce Comprehension:
Compare and Contrast

Compare and Contrast

Read the selection below and complete the Venn Diagram.

The whooping crane is the tallest bird in America. It stands about five feet tall, and its wings are almost seven feet long. It was named because of its loud whooping call. It is an endangered species. Scientists are working to save the whooping cranes.

There is only one wild flock of whooping cranes in the world. This flock spends its summers in northwest Canada nesting and raising their young. In the fall, the cranes migrate 2,400 miles to the coast of Texas. They spend the winter and early spring in Texas where it is warm. They return to Canada in the spring. In 2007, 236 cranes were in the wild flock.

In 2001, scientists formed a second migratory flock. This flock spends its summers in Wisconsin and migrates 1,240 miles to Florida. Since this flock was new, scientists put on costumes and used crane puppets to teach the birds how to migrate. The scientists used an ultralight aircraft because it can fly slowly enough for the birds to follow. It worked. Now the cranes are migrating on their own. In 2007, 55 adults and 17 chicks headed to Florida to spend the winter. It will take many years to see if this second flock survives.

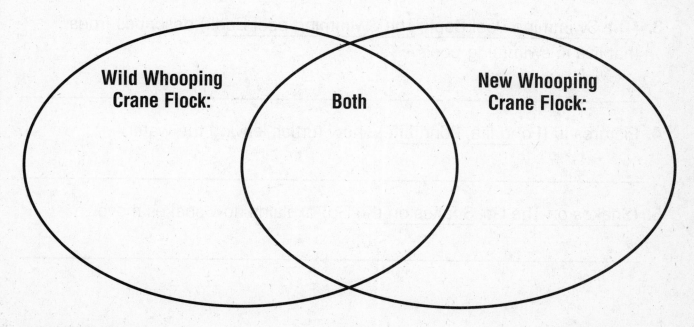

Wild Whooping
Crane Flock:

Both

New Whooping
Crane Flock:

Book Titles

- Begin the first, last, and each important word in a book title with a capital letter. Always underline a book title.

  We read about turtles migrating in <u>Reptiles on the Road</u>.

- *Reptiles* and *Road* are the first and last words of the title. The words *on* and *the* are not important words in the title.

Thinking Question
Is the word the first, the last, or an important word in the book title?

Write each sentence. Choose the correct book title.

1. I loved the book called (<u>Moving All the Time</u>, <u>Moving all the time</u>).

_____

2. (<u>reptiles On The run</u>, <u>Reptiles on the Run</u>) says reptiles run away from hurricanes.

_____

3. (<u>The Swimming Pool Book</u>, <u>The Swimming pool Book</u>) describes frogs that live in swimming pools.

_____

4. Pictures in (<u>Pond life</u>, <u>Pond Life</u>) show turtles leaving the water.

_____

5. (<u>Snakes on The Go</u>, <u>Snakes on the Go</u>) explains how snakes move.

_____

Spelling Word Sort

Write each Basic Word under the correct heading.

Words ending with -*es*	Words ending with -*ed*
_____	_____
_____	_____
_____	_____
_____	_____
_____	_____
_____	_____
_____	_____
_____	_____
_____	_____

Spelling Words

Basic
1. cities
2. cried
3. puppies
4. hurried
5. stories
6. flies
7. parties
8. tried
9. pennies
10. fried
11. carried
12. babies
13. spied
14. ponies

Review
pretty
very

Challenge
countries
libraries

Review: Suppose you were asked to add a column for the Review Words. What would you name the heading of that

column? _____

Challenge: Add the Challenge Words to your Word Sort.

Focus Trait: Word Choice
Using Similes

Description	Simile Added
My face turned red.	My face turned as red as a tomato.

A. Read each description. Create a clearer picture by adding a simile using *like* or *as*.

Description	Simile Added
1. Huge rain clouds blocked the sun and made it dark outside.	Huge rain clouds blocked the sun and made _____.
2. The children walking in the hallway are loud.	The children walking in the hallway are _____ _____.

B. Read each description. Add a simile to each description to create a clearer picture for the reader. Write your new sentences.

Pair/Share Work with a partner to brainstorm similes to add to each description.

Description	Simile Added
3. The freshly washed floor was slippery.	
4. The new mall is huge.	

Less Common Plurals

Read each sentence. Choose the missing word from
the box. Write the word. Then reread each complete sentence.

knives
leaves
hooves
lives
loaves

1. The blacksmith put shoes on the horses'

_____.

2. Run for your _____! The volcano is erupting!

3. Do you have any _____ of wheat bread?

4. In autumn, the _____ fall from the trees.

5. Set the table with forks, _____, and spoons.

Lesson 22
PRACTICE BOOK

**The Journey:
Stories of Migration**
Deepen Comprehension:
Compare and Contrast

Compare and Contrast

Read the selection below.

There are five oceans on Earth, and the Arctic Ocean is the smallest. It lies between Europe, Asia, and North America in the Arctic Circle.

Like all oceans, the Arctic is made of water. But, this is water you can walk on! Much of the Arctic Ocean is frozen. There are very thick icebergs on parts of the Arctic Ocean.

Winters and summers in the Arctic are quite different. The summers are damp and foggy. There is daylight all the time—both day and night are filled with light. The sun never sets in the summer in the Arctic. Sometimes this area is called "The Land of the Midnight Sun."

Winters are a time of darkness. The sun never rises. It is dark all the time. The weather is much colder in the winter and the skies are usually clear.

On a separate sheet of paper, complete a Venn Diagram to show the details compared and contrasted in the text. Then answer the questions below.

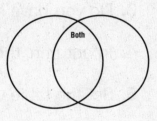
Both

1. What signal words does the author use to show this is a compare-contrast text structure?

   _____

2. How are the seasons in the Arctic Ocean alike and different? Use text details to support your answer.

   _____

   _____

   _____

Lesson 22
PRACTICE BOOK

**The Journey:
Stories of Migration**
Grammar:
Using Proper Nouns

Titles of People

**Underline the official title of a person in each sentence.
Then write the sentence correctly.**

1. Last night, aunt Lola told me that some animals migrate.

_____

_____

2. Then uncle Peter said animals that migrate move from place to place.

_____

_____

3. The next day, principal East showed us a film.

_____

_____

4. First, coach Greene told us that it was about animals.

_____

_____

5. A man named doctor Brown talked about each animal.

_____

_____

6. After the film, superintendent Jones talked to us.

_____

_____

Lesson 22
PRACTICE BOOK

**The Journey:
Stories of Migration**
Spelling:
Changing Final *y* to *i*

Changing Final *y* to *i*

Write the Basic Word or Words to answer each question.

1. Which word names big places? _____

2. Which words name living things?

   _____, _____,

   _____, _____

3. Which words rhyme with lied?

   _____, _____,

   _____, _____

4. Which word names money you can carry in a pocket?

   _____

5. Which verb names what you did when you were late

   to something? _____

6. What words make you think of food?

   _____, _____

7. Which word names things that you read?

   _____

8. Write two words that name something small.

   _____, _____

Review Name two words that are adjectives. _____, _____

Challenge Write two words that name places. _____, _____

Spelling Words

Basic
1. cities
2. cried
3. puppies
4. hurried
5. stories
6. flies
7. parties
8. tried
9. pennies
10. fried
11. carried
12. babies
13. spied
14. ponies

Review
pretty
very

Challenge
countries
libraries

Prefixes *in-*, *im-*

Read each question. Use the underlined word to write a complete sentence to answer each question.

1. Why might someone <u>immigrate</u> to this country?

_____

_____

2. How could you make an <u>imprint</u> of your hand in a piece of clay?

_____

_____

3. What can you play <u>indoors</u>?

_____

_____

4. How do you <u>input</u> information into a computer?

_____

_____

5. What is your favorite thing to find <u>inside</u> a lunchbox?

_____

_____

6. What kinds of things do we <u>import</u> from other countries?

_____

_____

Name _____ Date _____

Lesson 22
PRACTICE BOOK

The Journey:
Stories of Migration
Grammar:
Spiral Review

Correct Adjectives

- The words *a*, *an*, and *the* are special adjectives called
  articles. Use *a* and *an* with singular nouns. Use *a*
  before words that begin with a consonant sound.
  Use *an* before words that begin with a vowel sound.
  Use *the* before both singular and plural nouns.
- An adjective formed from a proper noun should
  begin with a capital letter.

  The class took **a** bus to see **an** exhibit of
  African zebras.

1–2. Rewrite each sentence correctly. Capitalize proper adjectives.

1. We also saw european deer.

_____

2. A irish scientist gave a talk.

_____

3–6. Use proofreading marks to write *a*, *an*, and *the* correctly.

Dear Diary,

   We took a trip to see butterflies. We also saw a ant as big as a spider.

An guide told us about butterflies in Mexico. He described the stages of an

butterfly's life. I asked him an question, and he answered it.

                              Ken

Lesson 22
PRACTICE BOOK

**The Journey:
Stories of Migration**
Spelling:
Changing Final *y* to *i*

Proofreading for Spelling

Find and circle the misspelled words.

> When I help Ms. Mancia in the library, I have spyed many funny things. I made a list of some of them.
>
> • Two pennys were found in a book about banking!
>
> • Once a man carryed four babies in at one time. He held all four while he looked something up on the computer. Then he hurreed out.
>
> • Two flis landed on a book titled *Insect Homes*.
>
> • A girl cried as she looked at pictures of puppyes.
>
> • There were two parties on Valentine's Day that both served fryed chicken. Chicken on Valentine's Day?
>
> • A woman driving a truck filled with apples from a farm asked, "Do you have any storys about California cites?"
>
> • Two ponies tryd to climb in through a window. Okay, I made that one up!

Spelling Words

1. cities
2. cried
3. puppies
4. hurried
5. stories
6. flies
7. parties
8. tried
9. pennies
10. fried
11. carried
12. babies
13. spied
14. ponies

Review
pretty
very

Challenge
countries
libraries

Write the misspelled words correctly on the lines below.

1. _____   6. _____

2. _____   7. _____

3. _____   8. _____

4. _____   9. _____

5. _____   10. _____

Name _____ Date _____

Lesson 22
PRACTICE BOOK

**The Journey:
Stories of Migration**
Grammar:
Connect to Writing

Ideas

Using proper noun phrases helps the reader better understand when the events occur.

Sentences	Clearer Sentence
Last week we visited the aquarium.	Last week, on Saturday, we visited the aquarium.
We started our project.	We started our project on Tuesday.

Write each sentence. Add the proper nouns and any other words in parentheses.

1. My father took out our boat. (last Monday)

_____

2. We looked for whales. (on Saturday)

_____

3. Every weekend we watched sea creatures. (in August)

_____

4. My father told us animal stories. (on Father's Day)

_____

5. Next week we are going on a trip. (on Friday)

_____

Name _____ Date _____

Lesson 23
PRACTICE BOOK

The Journey of
Oliver K. Woodman
Phonics: Suffixes
-ful, -y, -ous, -ly, -er

Suffixes -ful, -y, -ous, -ly, -er

**Read each sentence. Choose the missing word from the box.
Write the word. Then reread the complete sentence.**

spoonful	messy	islander
runner	closely	windy
nervous	bravely	
graceful	joyous	

1. The _____ weather blew the hat right off my head!

2. The first _____ of soup is the hottest.

3. The _____ dancer crossed the stage and leaped into the air.

4. Damian _____ walked across the swinging bridge while
Cassidy nervously stayed behind.

5. The _____ sells coconuts and pineapples on the beach.

6. The lamb followed _____ behind the mother sheep so it
wouldn't get lost.

7. My _____ dog spilled her dog food and tracked mud across
the floor.

8. It was a _____ occasion at my house when I brought home
a good report card.

9. Do you feel _____ about singing the solo in the school play?

10. When the _____ crossed the finish line, she held her hands
over her head in celebration.

Abbreviations for Days and Months

> • An **abbreviation** is a short way to write a word.
> Most abbreviations begin with capital letters
> and end with periods.
>
> Monday; August
>
> Mon.; Aug.

Thinking Question
*Is the word a day of
the week or a month
of the year?*

Write the correct abbreviation for each day and month.

1. Sunday _____

2. December _____

3. Tuesday _____

4. Thursday _____

5. Saturday _____

6. November _____

7. Wednesday _____

8. September _____

9. Friday _____

10. February _____

Lesson 23
PRACTICE BOOK

**The Journey of
Oliver K. Woodman**

Introduce Comprehension:
Sequence of Events

Sequence of Events

Read the selection below.

On Monday, Lily walked into the garage where her father was working. She liked to watch him build things. Dad drilled holes in the top and bottom of an oval-shaped piece of wood.

On Wednesday evening, Lily watched her dad sand something shaped like a small mitten. Lily noticed pieces on a table that looked like a body, arms, legs, and a head. "What are you making?"

"It's a marionette," Dad said holding up two tiny wooden shoes. "You can help me tie string through the holes to attach the arms and legs to the body."

Once the figure was tied together, Dad held it by the strings and it hung down to the floor. He pulled one string and the doll lifted its leg. He pulled another and it lifted its arm. Lily laughed. Dad showed her how to move the strings to make it dance.

Over the next few days. Lily made a fancy hat and a dress out of cloth. She named the marionette "Fancy."

Complete the Flow Chart to show the sequence of events.

[ ]
↓
[ ]
↓
[ ]
↓
[ ]

Name _____ Date _____

Lesson 23
PRACTICE BOOK

**The Journey of
Oliver K. Woodman**

Grammar:
Abbreviations

Abbreviations for Places

- An **abbreviation** is a short way to write a word.
- Places whose names can be abbreviated include roads, streets, lanes, avenues, and boulevards. Examples include *Harrison Rd.*, *Maple St.*, *Elmira Ln.*, *Plainville Ave.*, and *Broad Blvd.*

Thinking Question
Is the word the name of a place?

Write each place name correctly. Use capital letters and abbreviations.

1. King Boulevard _____

2. Jefferson Street _____

3. Western Avenue _____

4. Oak Road _____

5. Chestnut Lane _____

6. Elm Boulevard _____

7. Washington Street _____

8. Smith Lane _____

9. Vermont Avenue _____

10. Lincoln Street _____

Spelling Word Sort

Write each Basic Word under the correct heading.

Lesson 23
PRACTICE BOOK

**The Journey of
Oliver K. Woodman**
Spelling:
The Suffixes *-ful*, *-ly*, and *-er*

Words that End with the Suffix *-ful*	Words that End with the Suffix *-ly*
_____	_____
_____	_____
_____	_____
_____	_____
_____	_____
_____	_____

Words that End with the Suffix *-er*	
_____	_____
_____	_____

Review   Add the Review Words to your Word Sort.

Challenge   Add the Challenge Words to your Word Sort.

Spelling Words

Basic
1. singer
2. loudly
3. joyful
4. teacher
5. fighter
6. closely
7. powerful
8. farmer
9. quickly
10. careful
11. friendly
12. speaker
13. wonderful
14. truly

Review
hopeful
safely

Challenge
listener
calmly

Focus Trait: Voice
Showing Characters' Feelings

Instead of this...	*...a writer wrote this to show feelings.*
Wendy is a good friend.	Wendy is a fun girl to spend a Saturday afternoon with!

A. Read the sentence. Rewrite the sentence to show your feelings.

Instead of this...	*...the author wrote this to show feelings.*
1. I liked the food.	_____

B. Read each event from *The Journey of Oliver K. Woodman*. Look at the pictures on the pages listed below. Write a line of dialogue in which Oliver shows how he might have felt.

Pair/Share Work with a partner to brainstorm words that show feelings.

Event	Dialogue with Feelings
2. Oliver rode with three sisters. (pp. 250–251)	
3. Oliver got to Tameka's house. (pp. 254–255)	

Name _____ Date _____

Lesson 23
PRACTICE BOOK

The Journey of
Oliver K. Woodman

Phonics:
Cumulative Review

Cumulative Review

**Read each sentence. Choose the missing word from the box.
Write the word. Then reread the complete sentence.**

salty	handful	numerous
juicy	baker	happily
beautiful	butcher	
finely	dangerous	

1. There are _____ kinds of snacks, and there are many healthful ones to choose from.

2. A _____ of raisins is a good snack. You can grab them and go!

3. Some people like _____ snacks like pretzels or nuts.

4. A _____ can make muffins and breads.

5. Not only do bakeries smell good but the items are _____ to look at.

6. _____ chopped vegetables make a good snack. Put the small pieces of carrot or celery on a salad, cracker, or slice of cheese.

7. There is nothing like a _____ orange as a snack. You can eat it or squeeze it into a glass and drink it!

8. A knife is a _____ tool. The sharp edge could cut a child's fingers.

9. A _____ is trained in how to use a knife. His job is to cut meat using very sharp tools.

10. After your snack, smile and go _____ on with your day!

Name _____ Date _____

Lesson 23
PRACTICE BOOK

The Journey of Oliver K. Woodman
Deepen Comprehension:
Sequence of Events

Sequence of Events

Read the selection below.

One January afternoon my piano teacher, Ms. North, handed me sheet music for a new song called "Tanya's Song." I laughed because my name is Tanya. It was a difficult piece. "I think you should perform it at the Spring Show on March 2," Ms. North said.

I sat at the piano and tried to play it. I played the fast parts really slow. I made many mistakes playing the slow parts. When Ms. North left, she said one word. "Practice."

After two weeks, I played the song much better, but I still had trouble.

With just one week to go before the show, my fingers hurt. I couldn't get the song out of my head.

Finally, the first of March arrived. Ms. North sat beside me on the piano bench and said, "I have to tell you about this song. I wrote it. I knew you could play it better than anyone else, so I named it for you."

The next day, I sat at the piano. I could see my family sitting beside Ms. North. I felt the swirling notes come out of my fingers. It really felt like this was my song. I played it beautifully! All my practice paid off!

On a separate sheet of paper, complete a Flow Chart with the sequence of events. Then answer the questions below.

1. What signal words does the author use to show the sequence of events in the story?

_____

_____

2. What did Tanya do that helped her play the song so well?

_____

_____

Name _____ Date _____

Lesson 23
PRACTICE BOOK

The Journey of
Oliver K. Woodman
Grammar:
Abbreviations

Writing Abbreviations

1–5. Write the correct abbreviation for each day and month.

1. Tuesday _____

2. January _____

3. Friday _____

4. October _____

5. Saturday _____

6–10. Abbreviate each place name correctly.

6. Myer Lane _____

7. Hudson Street _____

8. Prospect Road _____

9. Lynn Boulevard _____

10. North Avenue _____

Lesson 23
PRACTICE BOOK

The Journey of
Oliver K. Woodman
Spelling:
The Suffixes *-ful*, *-ly*, and *-er*

The Suffixes *-ful*, *-ly*, and *-er*

Write a Basic Word to complete each sentence.

1. A person singing in a choir is a _____.

2. If your friends yell during a game, they are playing _____.

3. A person who grows corn in the country is a _____.

4. If you run fast, you are moving _____.

5. If you are very happy, you are _____.

6. The person whose desk is in the front of your classroom is your _____.

7. Someone who is very strong is _____.

8. When you use scissors, you should be _____.

9. A person who smiles and asks you how you are feeling is _____.

10. If you do not lie to someone, you are speaking _____.

Review: Choose a Review Word that completes the sentence.

If you want something to happen, you are _____.

Challenge: Choose a Challenge Word. Use it in a sentence.

_____

Spelling Words

Basic
1. singer
2. loudly
3. joyful
4. teacher
5. fighter
6. closely
7. powerful
8. farmer
9. quickly
10. careful
11. friendly
12. speaker
13. wonderful
14. truly

Review
hopeful
safely

Challenge
listener
calmly

Lesson 23
PRACTICE BOOK

The Journey of Oliver K. Woodman
Vocabulary Strategies:
Suffixes -er, -est

Suffixes -er, -est

Read the paragraph. Circle the words with the suffix -er or -est. Then write the base words on the lines below.

Saturday was the loveliest, sunniest day we had all week, but I had to go to my first piano lesson. The teacher, Mrs. Spindle, was older than I had expected. But she was also kinder. She served tea and cookies, and then we started the lesson. Reading and playing music was harder than I had imagined. But I felt happier after the lesson than I had before.

1. _____   4. _____

2. _____   5. _____

3. _____   6. _____

Use the base word to create a word with the suffix -er or -est. Complete the sentence.

7. **nice:** Mr. Beale is the _____ teacher in the world!

8. **dark:** The sky is _____ tonight than it was last night.

9. **strange:** This is the _____ book I have ever read!

10. **young:** My cousin is two years _____ than I am.

Name _____ Date _____

Lesson 23
PRACTICE BOOK

The Journey of
Oliver K. Woodman
Grammar:
Spiral Review

The Special Verb *be*

- The verbs *am*, *is*, *are*, *was*, and *were* are forms of the verb *be*. They do not show action. They tell what someone or something is or was. *Am*, *is*, and *are* show present tense. *Was* and *were* show past tense.

  The trip **is** fun.   The trip **was** fun.

1–3. Write the verb. Write *present* or *past* for each verb.

1. The boys are tired of the traveling. _____

2. We were in ten states. _____

3. I am ready to go on another trip. _____

4–6. Combine two short sentences by moving one predicate to make one longer sentence with two predicates. Write the new sentence on the line.

4. Father is a good driver. Father is tired of driving.

_____

5. We are out of the car. We are ready to relax.

_____

6. Mother and Jorge are happy. Mother and Jorge are in the house.

_____

Proofreading for Spelling

Read the following letter. Circle the misspelled words.

Dear Marcus,

My class heard a speeker today. His name was Mr. Brown. He showed us pictures of different parts of the country. We saw a picture of a farmar on his farm. I looked at the picture closelie to see all the animals.

We saw pictures of the Rocky Mountains. What a wunderful trip that would be! I am hopefull that someday I will see the mountains.

Some of my friends were talking lowdley. Mrs. Garcia told them to be quiet. Mrs. Garcia is our teachur.

Mr. Brown answered all of our questions. He was very frenly.

After the speech, we all went kuikly back to our classrooms. I was carefull not to bump into anyone on the way.

Your friend,
Danny

Spelling Words

1. singer
2. loudly
3. joyful
4. teacher
5. fighter
6. closely
7. powerful
8. farmer
9. quickly
10. careful
11. friendly
12. speaker
13. wonderful
14. truly

Review
hopeful
safely

Challenge
listener
calmly

Write the misspelled words correctly on the lines below.

1. _____
2. _____
3. _____
4. _____
5. _____
6. _____
7. _____
8. _____
9. _____
10. _____

Lesson 23
PRACTICE BOOK

**The Journey of
Oliver K. Woodman**
Grammar:
Connect to Writing

Conventions: Proofreading

Proofreading your work for correctly spelled
abbreviations will make your writing stronger.

Incorrect Abbreviation	Correct Abbreviation
tues; mar	Tues.; Mar.
ln; rd	Ln.; Rd.

**Use proofreading marks to write abbreviations correctly in this
informal note.**

Sun, Oct 3

Liam,

    We stopped by Pleasant Str on fri and met your uncle's family. He is a

wonderful man, and his kids and wife are great, too. We met Pat Smith, who

is very nice. He lives in Miami, too. He has a house on Beach Blvd near the

ocean. We are going to meet him and Cindy Birch next Tues for a clambake.

                           Lucy

Proofreading Marks
¶ Indent
∧ Add
⌐ Delete
≡ Capital letter
/ Small letter

Lesson 24
PRACTICE BOOK

Dog-of-the-Sea-Waves
Phonics: Prefixes
un-, pre-, re-, bi-

Prefixes *un-, pre-, re-, bi-*

**Read each sentence. Choose the missing word from the box.
Write the word. Then reread the complete sentence.**

refilled	preview	unsafe	unbroken
preheat	unopened	biweekly	bicycle
redo	pretest		

1. Did you see the old _____ fly by?

2. It is _____ to run on an icy sidewalk.

3. The movie _____ showed funny parts of the
new movie.

4. I only have to study the words I missed on the spelling

_____.

5. The _____ magazine comes out every
two weeks.

6. Mom _____ my glass after I finished the
first glass of juice.

7. I was so glad the vase was _____ after
I dropped it.

8. Tomas had to _____ the poster after he
misspelled a word on it.

9. I left the gifts _____ while I waited for my
sisters to come home.

10. The recipe says to _____ the oven to
325 degrees before putting the chicken in.

Adverbs That Tell *How*

- Words that describe verbs are called **adverbs**.

  On boat trips everything must work <u>perfectly</u>.

  We can <u>easily</u> fix things that break.
- Adverbs in these sentences tell *how*.
- Most adverbs that tell *how* end in *-ly*.
- Adverbs can come before or after the verbs they describe.

Thinking Question
What word tells how?

Write the adverb that tells *how* in each sentence.

1. The boat's rope broke suprisingly. _____

2. The boys worked quickly to fix it. _____

3. Jen cleverly made her own rope. _____

4. The rain poured heavily over the boat. _____

5. The captain politely told us to stay away. _____

6. She proudly steered the boat. _____

7. The captain watched her closely. _____

8. The wind pushed the sails wildly. _____

9. Everything was tied down tightly. _____

10. They arrived safely. _____

Author's Purpose

Read the selection below.

Kaimu Beach was the most famous black-sand beach on the island of
Hawaii. Thousands of people visited the beach to see the black sand.
Visitors swam and took many photographs. In 1990, all of that changed.
The island of Hawaii was formed by a volcano. Lava continues to flow
out of the volcano, but the hot, liquid rock flows out slowly. In 1989, the
volcano began to erupt. Lava destroyed a visitor center and some other
buildings. This was just a hint of what was to come.

In April 1990, a large lava flow came down from the volcano. It buried
the beach. It destroyed the beach hotels. Kaimu Beach was no more.

Today, the beach is filled with black rocks. New palm trees have been
planted and are beginning to grow. Black sand lies along the water's edge.
It forms when the seawater hits the hot lava and breaks it into tiny pieces.
The beating of the waves breaks it into fine pieces of sand. Maybe,
someday, Kaimu Beach will be filled with visitors again.

**Complete the Inference Map to show the author's purpose for
writing this selection.**

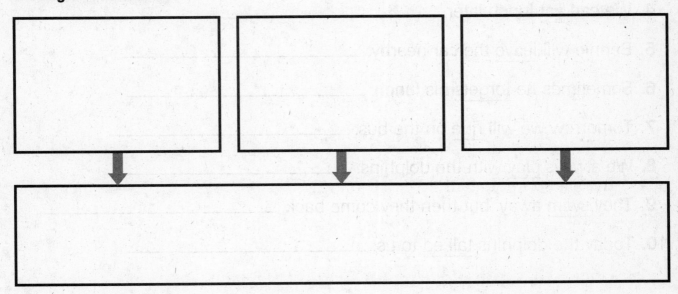

Dog-of-the-Sea-Waves
Grammar:
What Is an Adverb?

Adverbs That Tell
When and *Where*

- Adverbs tell *how*. They can also tell *when* and *where*.
- Adverbs can come before or after the verbs they describe.

  We went swimming with dolphins <u>there</u>.

  <u>Then</u> we watched the seals.

Thinking Question
Do the words tell
when *or* where?

Write the adverb that tells about each underlined verb. Then write
***when* or *where* for each adverb.**

1. The dolphins' swimming pool <u>lies</u> ahead. _____

2. First we will <u>watch</u> them swim. _____

3. Then we will <u>visit</u> more of the zoo. _____

4. We can <u>eat</u> lunch later. _____

5. Bennie will <u>leave</u> the car nearby. _____

6. Sometimes he <u>forgets</u> his lunch. _____

7. Tomorrow we will <u>ride</u> on the bus. _____

8. We always <u>play</u> with the dolphins. _____

9. They <u>swim</u> away, but then they come back. _____

10. Today the dolphins <u>talked</u> to us. _____

Spelling Word Sort

Dog-of-the-Sea Waves
Spelling:
The Prefixes *re*- and *un*-

Write each Basic Word under the correct heading.

Prefix that means "again"	Prefix that means "not" or "opposite of"

Review   Add the Review Words to your Word Sort.

Challenge   Add the Challenge Words to your Word Sort.

Spelling Words

Basic
1. unfold
2. rejoin
3. untie
4. reheat
5. unfair
6. unclear
7. repaid
8. rewrite
9. unhurt
10. recheck
11. unlucky
12. unwrap
13. reuse
14. unsure

Review
reread
unsafe

Challenge
unbuckle
unknown

Focus Trait: Ideas
Using Vivid Details

Good story writers use vivid details to paint a clear picture. Compare the sentence without vivid details to the one with vivid details.

Without Vivid Details: The beach was beautiful in the morning.

With Vivid Details: The sunrise cast a warm glow over the golden sands of the empty beach.

Rewrite each sentence, adding vivid details. You may use ideas from the box below or think of your own.

gently	sparkling	shady	cool

1. They had to cross the ocean to get home.

_____

2. Manu cleaned the animal's wound.

_____

3. He built a shelter from the sun.

_____

4. He gathered berries.

_____

5. He dived into the water.

_____

Cumulative Review

Read each sentence. Choose the missing word from the box. Write the word.

bimonthly	revisit	unequal	rebuild
reelected	preheat	unfriendly	unknown

1. I had so much fun at the park that I hope we _____ it next summer.

2. I asked Uncle Ramon to pour more juice into my glass because the amounts in the two glasses were _____.

3. Be sure to _____ the oven before you put the biscuits in to bake.

4. The mayor was _____ for a second term after all the votes were counted.

5. The _____ school newspaper comes out on the first and fifteenth of the month.

6. The _____ store clerk did not look up when I said hello.

7. There was no card on the flowers that were sent by an _____ person.

8. The carpenter had to _____ the bookshelves for a second time.

Author's Purpose

Read the selection below.

Scientist Thor Heyerdahl lived in the Polynesian Islands in the Pacific Ocean. He watched the way the winds blew and the ocean currents moved. He got an idea that the first people to live in Polynesia had come from South America.

Other scientists did not agree with Thor's ideas. Thor decided to prove that he was right.

In 1947, he built a raft. He named it *Kon-Tiki*. Thor and five crew members put the raft in the ocean in Peru, South America. They let the raft move by winds and ocean currents. After 101 days, the *Kon-Tiki* landed on a Polynesian island. The voyage was a success!

Thor wrote the book *Kon-Tiki* about the voyage. It sold millions of copies. Even a movie was made about the voyage.

On a separate sheet of paper, complete an Inference Map about the author's purpose. Then answer the questions.

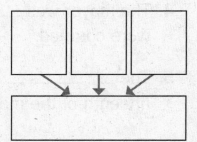

1. What was the author's purpose in writing this selection?

   _____

2. How would you describe Thor Heyerdahl? Support your answer with details from the text.

   _____

   _____

   _____

Comparing with Adverbs

Write each sentence. Use the correct form of the adverb in parentheses.

1. That dog is walking (slowly) than it used to walk.

   _____

2. Of all the birds I've heard, Jan's pet bird sings (sweetly).

   _____

3. Cats move (quietly) than dogs do.

   _____

4. She knew the answer (quickly) than I did.

   _____

5. Mice move (swiftly) than hamsters.

   _____

6. James listened (closely) of all to the whale songs.

   _____

7. The crowd clapped (excitedly) of all at the seal's tricks.

   _____

8. I worked (intently) on the report than she did.

   _____

The Prefixes *re-* and *un-*

Dog-of-the-Sea Waves
Spelling
The Prefixes *re-* and *un-*

Write a Basic Word to answer each clue.

1. You might do this with shoe laces. _____

2. You would do this to a present wrapped in paper.

   _____

3. You might feel this way if you didn't know the answer to

   a question. _____

4. To be sure your answers on a test were correct, you

   might do this. _____

5. If you thought someone had cheated in a game, you

   might think the game was this. _____

6. You could do this to make some leftover food warm

   again. _____

7. If you didn't like a poem you had written, you might do

   this to it. _____

8. You would do this to a shirt you found folded in a

   drawer. _____

Review: Choose a Review Word. Write a clue for it.

_____

Challenge: Choose a Challenge Word. Write a clue for it.

_____

Spelling Words

Basic
1. unfold
2. rejoin
3. untie
4. reheat
5. unfair
6. unclear
7. repaid
8. rewrite
9. unhurt
10. recheck
11. unlucky
12. unwrap
13. reuse
14. unsure

Review
reread
unsafe

Challenge
unbuckle
unknown

Name _____ Date _____

Lesson 24
PRACTICE BOOK

Dog-of-the-Sea-Waves
Vocabulary Strategies:
Words from Other Languages

Words from Other Languages

Read each question and notice the underlined word that came from a language other than English. Write an answer to the question that includes the underlined word.

1. What would you expect to see on a <u>safari</u>?

_____

_____

2. What do you like best about your favorite <u>pajamas</u>?

_____

_____

3. Do you know how to dance the <u>polka</u>, or have you seen anyone do that dance?

_____

_____

4. What kind of concert would you like to have a <u>ticket</u> to?

_____

_____

5. What is something fun to do at a <u>carnival</u>?

_____

_____

Irregular Verbs

> Some verbs have a special spelling to show past tense.
> They have another spelling when used with *has*, *have*,
> and *had*.
>
> | | |
> |---|---|
> | The friends **eat**. | He **grows** crops. |
> | The friends **ate**. | He **grew** crops. |
> | The friends **have eaten**. | He **has grown** crops. |

1–5. Write the correct past tense of the verb in parentheses to complete each sentence. The underlined verbs will help.

1. We <u>had</u> (saw, seen) all the seals at the zoo. _____

2. Watching them (take, took) all our time. _____

3. The children <u>have</u> (came, come) to see them, too. _____

4. The seal pool <u>has</u> (grown, grew) very big. _____

5. The zoo people (did, done) all the work. _____

6–10. Use proofreading marks to write each irregular verb in this letter correctly.

Dear Uncle Charlie,

I has written to tell you about our zoo trip. We take everything we needed for lunch. Everybody have seen wonderful things today. Many people have came here. The owners of the zoo have did a great thing.

Love,
Yolanda

Proofreading for Spelling

Dog-of-the-Sea Waves
Spelling:
The Prefixes *re-* and *un-*

Read each direction. Circle the misspelled words.

1. Set up your tent. First, unfolde the tent.

2. Next, unrap the tent ropes. You need the ropes to set up your tent.

3. If ropes are tied, you need to untye them.

4. Try to reus plastic bags while at camp. Do not throw them away.

5. Do not reheet drinks or food. See your camp leader.

6. Be sure to rejoyn your group after lunch.

7. Always walk with a friend. Walking alone at camp is unsaff.

8. Are you sure you have everything? You should rechek your bag.

Spelling Words

1. unfold
2. rejoin
3. untie
4. reheat
5. unfair
6. unclear
7. repaid
8. rewrite
9. unhurt
10. recheck
11. unlucky
12. unwrap
13. reuse
14. unsure

Review
reread
unsafe

Challenge
unbuckle
unknown

Write the misspelled words correctly on the lines below.

1. _____   5. _____

2. _____   6. _____

3. _____   7. _____

4. _____   8. _____

Sentence Fluency

Short, choppy sentences can be combined to make your writing smoother. Combine two sentences by moving an adverb.

Short Sentences	Longer, Smoother Sentences
Sam taught his cat. Sam cleverly taught it.	Sam cleverly taught his cat.
Dave played with his pet. Dave played with it happily.	Dave played with his pet happily.

Combine two short, choppy sentences by moving an adverb. Write the new sentence on the line.

1. Tara's dog swims with her. It swims with her cheerfully.

_____

2. Ernesto worked with his bird. He worked with it patiently.

_____

3. His bird flies away and returns to him. It flies away and returns to him quickly.

_____

4. Bennie's cat rides on his bike. It rides on his bike eagerly.

_____

5. Jorge's pet snake wraps around his arm. It wraps around his arm loosely.

_____

Suffixes *-less*, *-ness*, *-able*

Read each sentence. Choose the missing word from the box. Write the word. Then reread the complete sentence.

boneless	predictable	enjoyable	happiness
painless	weightless	shyness	softness
breakable	darkness		

1. Patricia's face turned red with _____ when she walked on the stage.

2. That story was so _____ that I guessed the ending.

3. Things float around in a _____ spaceship.

4. I needed a flashlight to see in the _____.

5. Since I didn't need a shot, my doctor's visit was _____.

6. Chris smiled and clapped at the end of the _____ movie.

7. Be careful not to drop the box because it contains _____ items.

8. Mr. Griffin said, "The children in my classroom have brought me much joy and _____."

9. When you eat _____ chicken there are no bones left on the plate!

10. Bradley sank back into the _____ of the pillow.

Name _____ Date _____

Lesson 25
PRACTICE BOOK

Mountains: Surviving on
Mt. Everest
Grammar:
What Is a Preposition?

What Is a Preposition?

Common Prepositions						
about	around	beside	for	near	outside	under
above	at	by	from	of	over	until
across	before	down	in	off	past	up
after	behind	during	inside	on	through	with
along	below	except	into	out	to	without

Underline the preposition in each sentence.

1. Some people like to hike the hills around a mountain.

2. Hiking over the hills is good exercise.

3. In summer, flowers cover the hills.

4. Some people like the mountains in winter.

5. They ski or snowboard down the steep slopes.

6. A high mountain is a challenge for climbers.

7. Reaching the top of a mountain is a climber's goal.

8. Climbers usually hike with a guide.

9. Guides know the safest way to the top.

10. Which mountains in our country have you seen?

Lesson 25
PRACTICE BOOK

**Mountains: Surviving on
Mt. Everest**
Introduce Comprehension:
Text and Graphic Features

Text and Graphic Features

Read the selection below.

What Is High-Altitude Sickness?

People can get sick just from going to high altitudes. It is called mountain sickness, or high-altitude sickness.

What happens

At higher altitudes, the air has less oxygen. Less oxygen goes to the lungs and brain. This can cause headaches, trouble breathing, an upset stomach, and a very tired feeling.

How to avoid this illness

The best way to avoid high-altitude sickness is to increase altitude slowly. Climbers should take two days to reach 8,000 feet. Next, they should rest and get used to the high altitude. Then, they can climb another 1,000 feet and wait again.

What to do if someone gets sick

If someone gets high-altitude sickness, he or she should get to a lower altitude right away. After resting, the body will adjust to the new altitude.

Complete the Column Chart to show the purpose of each text feature.

Feature	Location	Purpose

Name _____ **Date** _____

Lesson 25
PRACTICE BOOK

Mountains: Surviving on Mt. Everest
Grammar:
What Is a Preposition?

Prepositional Phrases

1–5. Underline the prepositional phrase in each sentence.

1. Those people in the distance are taking a hike.

2. I wonder how far they will hike before lunch?

3. We can follow the hikers up the hill.

4. My friend from the city likes hiking, too.

5. Let's hike to that tall pine tree.

6–10. Underline two prepositional phrases in each sentence. Write the prepositional phrase that tells *when***.**

6. On Friday, our class took a hike in the woods.

_____

7. I didn't think we were going on the hike until next week.

_____

8. We rested beside a creek at noon.

_____

9. During our rest, we looked at a distant mountain.

_____

10. By the afternoon, we were all very tired from the long hike.

_____

Name _____ Date _____

Spelling Word Sort

Write each Basic Word under the correct heading.

Suffix that means "without"	Suffix that means "quality of being"
_____	_____
_____	_____
_____	_____
_____	_____
_____	_____
_____	_____
_____	_____
_____	_____
_____	_____

Challenge   Add the Challenge Words to your Word Sort.

Spelling Words

Basic
1. painless
2. sickness
3. sadness
4. helpless
5. thankless
6. kindness
7. hopeless
8. darkness
9. fearless
10. thickness
11. careless
12. goodness
13. spotless
14. softness

Review
useful
weakly

Challenge
breathless
eagerness

Name _____ Date _____

Lesson 25
PRACTICE BOOK

Mountains: Surviving on
Mt. Everest
Writing:
Write to Express

Focus Trait: Word Choice
Choosing Strong Words

Without strong words: Very cold winds blew hard.

With strong words: Icy winds **roared by**.

Rewrite each sentence. Replace the underlined word or phrase with a stronger word or phrase from the box.

plunged	After nightfall	towering	terrible
fought	crush	summit	be wary of

1. Mt. Everest is a <u>very tall</u> mountain.

_____

2. Temba made a <u>bad</u> mistake and took off his gloves.

_____

3. <u>When it was dark</u>, the temperature <u>went way down</u>.

_____

4. Temba <u>worked hard</u> to reach the <u>top</u>.

_____

5. Climbers must <u>watch out for</u> huge pieces of ice that could
<u>fall on</u> them.

_____

Cumulative Review

Read each sentence. Choose the missing word from the box. Write the word. Then reread the complete sentence.

redo	sleepless	freshness	crispness
preview	erasable	tasteless	valuable

1. Justin spent a _____ night at the campout because he was worried about bears.

2. Take a bite of the celery and the crunch will tell you its _____.

3. The painting is _____ because it is one of a kind.

4. After one sip of the _____ soup, Tessa switched and ate something with more flavor.

5. I like to draw in pencil because it is _____, and I can fix my mistakes.

6. Daniel always smells each melon before buying it so he can test its

   _____.

7. I made so many mistakes, I had to _____ the whole assignment.

8. We got to _____ the movie before it came out in theaters.

Text and Graphic Features

Read the selection below.

Where Are High Mountains in the United States?

There are several in Alaska, California, and Colorado.

The Highest Peak in the U.S.

The highest peak in the U.S. is Mount McKinley in Alaska. It is 20,320 feet high. Alaska is home to the sixteen tallest peaks in the United States.

California's Mountains

The next highest mountain is in California. Mount Whitney stands a tall 14,491 feet.

Rocky Mountains

The tallest mountain in the Rocky Mountains is Mount Elbert in Colorado. It is 14,433 feet tall.

10 Tallest California Mountains	
Mountain Name	**Height**
1. Mount Whitney	14,491
2. Mount Williamson	14,370
3. White Mountain	14,246
4. North Palisade	14,242
5. Mount Shasta	14,162
6. Mount Sill	14,153
7. Mount Russell	14,088
8. Split Mountain	14,042
9. Mount Langley	14,022
10. Mount Tyndall	14,019

On a separate sheet of paper, complete a Column Chart about the text and graphic features. Then answer the questions.

1. What is the purpose of the three subheads?

   _____

   _____

2. How does the "California Mountains" chart connect to the text?

   _____

   _____

Lesson 25
PRACTICE BOOK

Mountains: Surviving on Mt. Everest
Grammar:
What Is a Preposition?

Prepositional Phrases

1–5. Underline the prepositional phrase in each sentence.

1. We use mountains for many things.

2. Rock climbers like to climb up mountain cliffs.

3. Miners search the rock for metals.

4. Some mountains supply logs for houses.

5. Cows and sheep can graze around a mountain's base.

6–10. Underline the prepositional phrases in each sentence. Write the prepositional phrase that tells *where*.

6. The weather on a mountain can change in a few minutes.

_____

7. It is very cold at the top of a mountain.

_____

8. At great heights, there is little oxygen for breathing.

_____

9. Many of the world's highest mountains are in Asia.

_____

10. Very few people live on these high mountains.

_____

Lesson 25
PRACTICE BOOK

Mountains: Surviving on
Mt. Everest
Spelling:
The Suffixes -*less* and -*ness*

The Suffixes -*less* and -*ness*

Write the Basic Word that makes sense in the sentence.

1. The hiker thanked the guide for her help and

_____ .

2. In high mountains, a lack of air can cause

_____ .

3. Being _____ in the mountains is
dangerous.

4. It is not wise to climb mountains in

_____ .

5. The _____ guide climbed the
high cliff.

6. I was amazed at the _____ of
the snow.

7. Scientists measured the _____ of
the ice at the top.

Challenge: Choose a Challenge Word. Use it in a sentence.

_____

Spelling Words

Basic
1. painless
2. sickness
3. sadness
4. helpless
5. thankless
6. kindness
7. hopeless
8. darkness
9. fearless
10. thickness
11. careless
12. goodness
13. spotless
14. softness

Review
useful
weakly

Challenge
breathless
eagerness

Name _____ Date _____

Lesson 25
PRACTICE BOOK

Mountains: Surviving on
Mt. Everest
Vocabulary Strategies:
Analogies

Analogies

Complete the analogies with a word from the box.

danger	increase	assist	departure
succeed	brave	slope	strength

1. Believable is to unbelievable as weakness is to _____.

2. Force is to power as achieve is to _____.

3. Polite is to rude as fearful is to _____.

4. Excellent is to wonderful as risk is to _____.

5. Frequent is to often as aid is to _____

6. Up is to down as arrival is to _____

7. Sad is to happy as decrease is to _____

8. Ocean is to wave as mountain is to _____

Name _____ Date _____

Lesson 25
PRACTICE BOOK

**Mountains: Surviving on
Mt. Everest**

Grammar:
Spiral Review

Contractions

> - Sometimes two words are put together and shortened to make a **contraction**. An apostrophe (') takes the place of any letter or letters left out.
> - Avoid using a contraction with *not* in a sentence that already has *not* or another negative word like *never*.

1–4. Write the contraction for the words in parentheses. Use an apostrophe in place of the underlined letters.

1. The boys _____ supposed to climb trees. (are n<u>o</u>t)

2. Torry says he _____ allowed to climb big trees. (is n<u>o</u>t)

3. His mom said she _____ think a small tree was a problem. (did n<u>o</u>t)

4. Torry promised he _____ climb too high. (would n<u>o</u>t)

5–8. Write the contraction for the words in parentheses. Use an apostrophe in place of the underlined letters.

5. The girls say _____ never climb a tree. (they w<u>ill</u>)

6. The boys answer that _____ got to try it. (they h<u>a</u>ve)

7. _____ try it to see if we like it. (We w<u>ill</u>)

8. _____ never had so much fun. (I h<u>a</u>ve)

Proofreading for Spelling

Read each journal entry. Circle the misspelled words.

Journal of a Mountain Guide

Monday: We rescued a hiker who had become lost in the darkniss.

Tuesday: It is hopless to teach some people how to be careful in the mountains. They just don't pay attention.

Wednesday: We took a short hike to the ranger station. It was paneless.

Thursday: Felt a strange softnes in my leg. I'll have a doctor check it tomorrow. Also checked the thikness of the ice on the trail. It's safe.

Friday: Found a hammer and some rope in the snow. Some careluss hiker must have dropped them.

Saturday: Some hikers thanked us for our kineness. I guess being a mountain guide is not always a thankliss job!

Spelling Words

Basic
1. painless
2. sickness
3. sadness
4. helpless
5. thankless
6. kindness
7. hopeless
8. darkness
9. fearless
10. thickness
11. careless
12. goodness
13. spotless
14. softness

Review
useful
weakly

Challenge
breathless
eagerness

Write the misspelled words correctly on the lines below.

1. _____   5. _____

2. _____   6. _____

3. _____   7. _____

4. _____   8. _____

Sentence Fluency

Short, choppy sentences can be combined to make
your writing smoother. You can combine two sentences
by **moving a prepositional phrase**.

Two Sentences	Combined Sentence
We watched the film about mountains. We watched the film on Tuesday.	We watched the film about mountains on Tuesday.

**Combine two short choppy sentences by moving a prepositional phrase
to combine two sentences. Write the new sentence on the line.**

1. The map is on the wall.

   The map is behind Mrs. Brown's desk.

   _____

2. We can see the mountains in Asia.

   We can see the mountains on the map.

   _____

3. Please, show me the mountains of North America.

   Please, show me the mountains on the map.

   _____

4. We will learn more about mountains.

   We will learn more after lunch.

   _____

5. Have you ever hiked in the mountains?

   Have you ever hiked in our state?

   _____

Lesson 26
PRACTICE BOOK

**The Foot Race
Across America**
Phonics: Common Final
Syllables *-ion, -tion, -sion, -ture*

Common Final Syllables

Choose a word from the box to complete each sentence.
Read the completed sentence.

Word Bank
action   attention   confusion   discussion   furniture
future   motion   nature   picture   protection

1. With this camera I will take your _____ .

2. No one knew what to do, so there was a lot of _____ .

3. If you push the toy car, you set it in _____ .

4. This is important news, so pay _____ .

5. Yesterday is the past, and tomorrow is the _____ .

6. If it's raining, an umbrella will give you _____ .

7. Let's talk about the plans in our _____ .

8. Tables, chairs, and sofas are kinds of _____ .

9. I like that pirate movie because it has plenty of _____ .

10. Trees, animals, and clouds are all parts of _____ .

Name _____ Date _____

Lesson 26
PRACTICE BOOK

The Foot Race
Across America
Spelling: Words with VCCV
Pattern

Words with the VCCV Pattern

Basic: Write the Basic Word that best fits each clue.

1. get pleasure from

2. an error

3. a human being

4. where flowers grow

5. opposite of remember

6. a baseball official

7. a command

8. protects your head

9. opposite of solution

10. soft floor covering

1. _____   6. _____

2. _____   7. _____

3. _____   8. _____

4. _____   9. _____

5. _____   10. _____

Challenge: Write two sentences about how you might
help a friend reach a goal. Use both of the Challenge Words.

_____

_____

_____

Spelling Words
Basic
1. person
2. helmet
3. until
4. carpet
5. Monday
6. enjoy
7. forget
8. problem
9. Sunday
10. garden
11. order
12. mistake
13. umpire
14. herself
Challenge
expect
wisdom

Word Sort

Write each Basic Word next to the correct heading.

Vowel *a* in first syllable	
Vowel *e* in first syllable	
Vowel *i* in first syllable	
Vowel *o* in first syllable	
Vowel *u* in first syllable	

Challenge: Add the Challenge Words to your Word Sort.

Spelling Words

Basic
1. person
2. helmet
3. until
4. carpet
5. Monday
6. enjoy
7. forget
8. problem
9. Sunday
10. garden
11. order
12. mistake
13. umpire
14. herself

Challenge
expect
wisdom

Lesson 26
PRACTICE BOOK

**The Foot Race
Across America**
Spelling: Words with VCCV
Pattern

Name _____ Date _____

Proofreading for Spelling

**Find the misspelled words and circle them. Write them
correctly on the lines below.**

Spelling Words

1. person
2. helmet
3. until
4. carpet
5. Monday
6. enjoy
7. forget
8. problem
9. Sunday
10. garden
11. order
12. mistake
13. umpire
14. herself

Some Really Super Softball

Last Sundy, the Braden Bobcats' fans got a big thrill
when the Bobcats beat the Pinehill Pumas.

The game was tied 1–1 in the last inning. The Bobcat
batters came up in ordor. First came Polly Peters, who
looked ready to win that game all by herrself. The Puma
pitcher, though, couldn't find the plate, and the umpeire
called four balls in a row. Polly walked to first base.

The next persen up to bat was Miko Myata. This time,
the Puma pitcher's probblem was wild pitches. When one
pitch hit Miko's helmit, Miko strolled to first base and Polly
moved to second.

The pitcher made one last misteak when he threw a
perfect pitch and Shayla Smith swung mightily. CRACK!
That ball was out of the park, and it probably didn't land
untill Munday. The Bobcats won it, 4–1!

1. _____   5. _____   9. _____

2. _____   6. _____   10. _____

3. _____   7. _____

4. _____   8. _____

Name _____ Date _____

Lesson 26
PRACTICE BOOK

The Foot Race
Across America
Grammar: Writing Quotations

Using Quotation Marks

- **Quotation marks (" ")** show the exact words a person says.
- Put quotation marks at the beginning and the end of the exact words someone says.

    Robert said, "I was determined to do well in the race."

Thinking Question
What are the exact words of a person?

Activity: Write each sentence correctly by adding quotation marks where needed.

1. Jen asked, What is your favorite thing to do outside?

   _____

   _____

2. Robert replied, I like to put on my running shoes and

   see how far I can run. _____

   _____

3. Jen said, I like running outside when it is sunny.

   _____

   _____

4. Robert asked, Have you ever been in a race?

   _____

   _____

5. Jen answered, I came in second in a race at school.

   _____

   _____

Name _____ Date _____

Lesson 26
PRACTICE BOOK

**The Foot Race
Across America**
Grammar: Writing Quotations

Quotations

- Use a **comma** to separate the speaker's exact words from the rest of the sentence.
- **Capitalize** the **first word** inside the quotation marks.
- Put the sentence **end mark** inside the quotation marks.

Thinking Question
What are the exact words of the speaker?

Activity: Write these sentences correctly. Add commas, capital letters, and end marks where they are needed.

1. Marco asked "when will the race start"

_____

2. Luis replied "the race will start when the runners are ready"

_____

3. Marco exclaimed "I can't wait for the race to begin"

_____

4. Luis said "the runners must work hard to get ready for the race"

_____

5. Luis added "they must run many miles every day"

_____

6. Marco said "I want to run in a race someday"

_____

Name _____ Date _____

Lesson 26
PRACTICE BOOK

The Foot Race
Across America
Grammar: Writing Quotations

Writing Quotations

Read each pair of sentences. Fill in the circle next to the sentence that uses correct punctuation.

1. Ⓐ Andy said, "Many of the runners became sick or tired."

   Ⓑ Andy said Many of the runners became sick or tired.

2. Ⓐ Gene exclaimed "Look at how fast that runner is going."

   Ⓑ Gene exclaimed, "Look at how fast that runner is going!"

3. Ⓐ His father "said, He had worked for this since he was a little boy."

   Ⓑ His father said, "He had worked for this since he was a little boy."

4. Ⓐ The man said, "It's amazing that one man can run that far."

   Ⓑ The man said, It's amazing that one man can run that far."

5. Ⓐ Look! "They're crossing the finish line now! shouted the boy.

   Ⓑ "Look! They're crossing the finish line now!" shouted the boy.

Name _____ Date _____

Possessive Nouns

- A **possessive noun** shows that a person or an animal owns or has something.
- To show that **one** person, place, or animal has possession, add an **apostrophe** and -s (*'s*).
- To show that **more than one** person, place, or animal has possession, add an -s and an **apostrophe** (*s'*).

Noun	Singular Possesive Noun	Plural Possessive Noun
teacher	teacher's	teachers'
runner	runner's	runners'

Activity: Write the word in parentheses as a possessive noun to complete the sentence.

1. _____ home is in Oklahoma. (Andy)

2. He runs in his _____ neighborhood. (cousin)

3. Andy likes to run with the _____ children. (neighbors)

4. He times his running with his _____ stopwatch. (sister)

5. The _____ prize is a huge trophy. (winner)

6. The _____ families all watched the race. (runners)

7. Allen could hear the _____ chirps as he ran. (bird)

8. Each _____ shirt had a number. (contestant)

9. Every runner could hear the _____ cheers. (fans)

10. The _____ statue of Andy shows him running. (town)

Word Choice: Words for *said*

Quotation with *Said*	Quotation with *Explained*
Marcus said, "Runners have to practice before a race, just as other athletes do."	Marcus explained, "Runners have to practice before a race, just as other athletes do."

Quotation with *Said*	Quotation with *Exclaimed*
Abigail said, "I'm so glad I got to see you run in the race today."	Abigail exclaimed, "I'm so glad I got to see you in the race today!"

Activity: Use the speaker's exact words to write a sentence that uses a verb other than *said*. Add quotation marks, commas, capital letters, and end marks as needed.

1.

Speaker	Exact Words
Derek	that was the most exciting race I have seen

_____

_____

2.

Speaker	Exact Words
Sheri	will you be in another race

_____

3.

Speaker	Exact Words
Luis	I will be running in a race next month

_____

Name _____ Date _____

Lesson 26
PRACTICE BOOK

The Foot Race
Across America
Writing: Organization

Focus Trait: Organization

Read each sentence that gives a comparing or contrasting detail. Write whether it compares or contrasts.

_____ Andy Payne and Peter Gavuzzi both competed in the International Trans-Continental Foot Race.

_____ Both men were called "Bunioneers."

_____ Andy was from Oklahoma, while Peter was from England.

_____ Andy won in 1928, but Peter won in 1929.

Think of a topic sentence for a paragraph that compares Andy and Peter. Write the sentence. Then write a topic sentence for a paragraph that contrasts Andy and Peter.

Comparing paragraph:

_____

_____

Contrasting paragraph:

_____

_____

Name _____ Date _____

Lesson 27
PRACTICE BOOK

**The Power
of Magnets**
Phonics: Double Consonants

Double Consonants

Choose a syllable from the left box and a syllable from the right box to make a word that completes each sentence. Write the word on the line, and read the completed sentence.

Hint: Each word you make will have a double consonant.

First Syllables					Second Syllables				
at	but	dol	fun	hap	den	der	lar	low	nel
lad	sud	tun	yel	zip	ny	pen	per	ter	tract

1. A magnet will _____ a nail.

2. What do you think will _____ next in that story?

3. Bonnie needs a _____ marker to color her sun picture.

4. I love peanut _____ sandwiches.

5. All of a _____ it started to rain.

6. I can't close my coat because the _____ is broken.

7. Climb up the _____ carefully.

8. That joke was so _____ that I hurt myself laughing.

9. Jake needs one more _____ to buy his lunch.

10. A mole will dig a _____ under the ground.

Double Consonants

Basic: Write the Basic Word that best completes each group.

1. sheet, blanket, _____

2. chapter, unit, _____

3. dime, quarter, _____

4. jam, preserves, _____

5. fox, raccoon, _____

6. top, side, _____

7. postcard, note, _____

8. peach, plum, _____

9. milk, cheese, _____

10. zipper, snap, _____

Challenge: Use one of the Challenge Words to write
a sentence.

_____

_____

_____

Spelling Words

Basic

1. jelly
2. bottom
3. pillow
4. happen
5. butter
6. lesson
7. cherry
8. sudden
9. arrow
10. dollar
11. hello
12. rabbit
13. letter
14. button

Challenge
stubborn
mirror

Name _____ Date _____

Word Sort

Write each Basic Word next to the correct heading.

Words with three letters in both syllables	
Words with two letters in one of their two syllables	
Words with four letters in both syllables	

Challenge: Add the Challenge Words to your Word Sort.

Spelling Words

Basic
1. jelly
2. bottom
3. pillow
4. happen
5. butter
6. lesson
7. cherry
8. sudden
9. arrow
10. dollar
11. hello
12. rabbit
13. letter
14. button

Challenge
stubborn
mirror

Name _____ Date _____

Proofreading for Spelling

**Find the misspelled words and circle them. Write them
correctly on the lines below.**

Dear Jamal,

Can you believe you're getting a leter from me, at
last? I think of you a lot, especially when I see a jar of that
charry jellie you love so much. Mom bought some the other
day, and all of a suddin, I find that I love it, too!

One of my front teeth fell out last week. I put the
tooth under my pilloaw. The next morning, a doller showed
up there. Maybe that's enough to buy a treat for my pet
rabit.

Hey, you're a science buff, right? Do you happan to
know much about magnets? We had a really neat lessone
on them in science class last week, and I'd love to talk to
you about them.

Well, say hellow to your family for me. Please write
back if you can. I miss you!

Your friend,

Curtis

Spelling Words
1. jelly
2. bottom
3. pillow
4. happen
5. butter
6. lesson
7. cherry
8. sudden
9. arrow
10. dollar
11. hello
12. rabbit
13. letter
14. button

1. _____   5. _____   9. _____

2. _____   6. _____   10. _____

3. _____   7. _____

4. _____   8. _____

Commas in Compound Sentences

- A **compound sentence** is a sentence made up of two complete sentences.
- A **connecting word** such as **and**, **but**, or **or** joins the sentences.
- A **comma** is used before the connecting word: Electricity comes through a wire, **and** it makes your lights work.

> **Thinking Question**
> Are there two complete sentences? What word is used to join the two sentences?

1–3. Write the sentence correctly with a comma.

1. Magnets can be used as decorations or they can be used to

make electricity. _____

_____

2. My favorite subject is science and I can't wait for the science fair.

_____

3. I want to use magnets in my science project but my partner

wants to do something else. _____

_____

4–5. Read each sentence. Decide if the sentence needs a comma. Write the sentence.

4. Small magnets decorate refrigerators but big magnets move cars.

_____

5. I always have a light on when I read and when I watch television.

_____

Commas with Dates and Places

The Power of Magnets
Grammar: Commas in Sentences

- A **comma** in a date separates the month and day from the year.
- A **comma** in a place separates the city or town and its state.

  I am driving to Madison, Wisconsin.
  I will get there on December 2, 2008.

Thinking Question
Does the sentence contain a date? Does it contain a city or town and its state?

1–5. Write these sentences correctly. Add a comma in the dates and places.

1. Manuel was born October 18 2000.

_____

2. Manuel and his family lived in Albany New York.

_____

3. His family moved on June 3 2007.

_____

4. They moved to a warmer climate in Dallas Texas.

_____

5. Manuel has a sister who was born February 20 2004.

_____

6–10. Fill in the correct date or place to complete each sentence. Remember to add commas where they belong.

6. I was born _____.(month, date, year)

7. I have been to _____.(city and state)

8. I live in _____.(city and state)

9. Today's date is _____.(month, date, year)

10. I want to go to _____.(city and state)

Name _____ Date _____

Lesson 27
PRACTICE BOOK

The Power of Magnets
Grammar: Commas in Sentences

Commas in Sentences

Read each pair of sentences. Fill in the circle next to the sentence that uses correct punctuation.

1. Ⓐ Magnets help make electricity, and they hold papers on a refrigerator.

   Ⓑ Magnets help make electricity and they hold papers on a refrigerator.

2. Ⓐ This winter we are going skiing in Vail Colorado.

   Ⓑ This winter we are going skiing in Vail, Colorado.

3. Ⓐ The last time it rained that much was, April 10 2006.

   Ⓑ The last time it rained that much was April 10, 2006.

4. Ⓐ Jack wrote about electricity for his science report, and he did research on lightning.

   Ⓑ Jack wrote about electricity for his science report and, he did research on lightning.

5. Ⓐ Lightning struck that tree on March, 6 2008.

   Ⓑ Lightning struck that tree on March 6, 2008.

Writing Proper Nouns

- A **proper noun** always begins with a capital letter.
- Days, months, holidays, historical periods, and special events are proper nouns.
- The first, last, and important words in a book title are capitalized. Book titles are underlined.

Proper Nouns	
Day	Wednesday
Month	March
Holiday	Thanksgiving
Book Title	The Giver

Activity: Write all proper nouns and book titles from each sentence correctly.

1. The electricity was turned off on friday. _____

2. I read the book, the haunted mansion, with a flashlight.

   _____

3. We saved a lot of electricity in june. _____

4. My book report on Michael Faraday is due after columbus day. _____

5. I would rather learn about world war II than about electricity. _____

6. My sister wants to write a book called when the lights go out _____

Sentence Fluency: Combining Sentences into Compound Sentences

Short, Choppy Sentences	Combined with *and*
Turning on lights uses electricity. Turning off lights saves electricity	Turning on lights uses electricity, and turning off lights saves electricity.

Activity: Write each pair of sentences as one sentence.
Use the word in ( ) to combine the sentences.

1. The flashlight was bright. The lantern was brighter. (but)

   _____

2. I use a lamp when I read magazines. I use a flashlight when I read mysteries. (but) _____

   _____

3. Josiah read that he can use a magnet to pick up pins. He is excited to see if it works. (and) _____

   _____

4. The photos and papers on our refrigerator are held up by magnets. They would fall off without the magnets. (and)

   _____

   _____

5. It might be hard to find interesting magnets for your refrigerator. You could always make some. (but)

   _____

   _____

Focus Trait: Ideas

Read each problem and solution. Add details to elaborate. Explain how the problem was solved and how the solution works. Use information from "The Power of Magnets."

1.   **Problem:** Kaylie dropped a box of pins.
     Solution: She used a magnet.
Details:

_____

_____

2.   **Problem:** The CD player does not work.
     Solution: We put a battery in it.
Details:

_____

_____

3.   **Problem:** A junkyard owner needs to move a car.
     Solution: He flips a switch.
Details:

_____

_____

4.   **Problem:** Michael Faraday wanted to produce electricity.
     Solution: He moved a magnet through a coil of wire.
Details:

_____

_____

Name _____ Date _____

Lesson 28
PRACTICE BOOK

Becoming Anything
He Wants to Be
Phonics: Words with
ough and *augh*

Words with *ough*, *augh*

Read each word in the box. Say the sound that *ough* or *augh* makes. Then write the word in the chart under the word that *ough* or *augh* rhymes with.

Word Bank					
bought	caught	fought	naughty	rough	taught
brought	daughter	laugh	ought	sought	thought

ough rhymes with *paw*	*ough* rhymes with *puff*	*augh* rhymes with *paw*	*augh* rhymes with *staff*

Words with *ough* and *augh*

Basic: Write the Basic Word that completes each sentence.

1. A mother and her _____ had a problem.

2. The little girl had _____ a bad cold.

3. Every day, the child's _____ grew worse.

4. Her sore throat made her voice _____ and scratchy.

5. The girl couldn't sleep _____ the night.

6. The mother knew she _____ to take the girl to a doctor.

7. They didn't have _____ money, though, to pay the bill.

8. Then the mother _____ of something.

9. Some of her neighbors had _____ to have a free clinic set up nearby.

10. So she picked up her daughter and _____ her to the clinic.

Challenge: Write a sentence about a problem you had and how you solved it. Use both Challenge Words.

_____

_____

_____

Spelling Words

Basic
1. taught
2. thought
3. rough
4. laugh
5. bought
6. cough
7. ought
8. caught
9. fought
10. daughter
11. tough
12. through
13. enough
14. brought

Challenge
sought
naughty

Name _____ Date _____

Lesson 28
PRACTICE BOOK

**Becoming Anything
He Wants to Be**

Spelling: Words with
ough and *augh*

Word Sort

Write each Basic Word beside the correct heading.

Words in which the letters *gh* are not pronounced	
Words in which the letters *gh* are pronounced /f/	

Spelling Words

Basic
1. taught
2. thought
3. rough
4. laugh
5. bought
6. cough
7. ought
8. caught
9. fought
10. daughter
11. tough
12. through
13. enough
14. brought

Challenge
sought
naughty

Challenge: Add the Challenge Words to your Word Sort.

Proofreading for Spelling

Becoming Anything He Wants to Be

Spelling: Words with *ough* and *augh*

Find the misspelled words and circle them. Write them correctly on the lines below.

Spelling Words
1. taught
2. thought
3. rough
4. laugh
5. bought
6. cough
7. ought
8. caught
9. fought
10. daughter
11. tough
12. through
13. enough
14. brought

Not long ago, our old dog, Bella, stopped coming when we called her. At first, we thouht she just wanted to show us who was boss. After all the training she'd had, though, she aught to know better.

Then the vet found Bella's problem: she had lost her hearing. We worried that Bella would have a tuff time in a silent world. That sweet girl, though, has tawght us a thing or two!

First, we baught a book about living with a deaf dog. We read throogh it carefully. We learned to talk to Bella with body signals, not our voices. In a few days, using an arm to beckon her brout her to us right away. When it was time for a walk, we held up a leash for her to see. That was ennough to get her racing to the door!

Today, we luagh to think we ever worried about Bella. She fougt to overcome her problem, and she's an even more amazing dog now.

1. _____   5. _____   8. _____

2. _____   6. _____   9. _____

3. _____   7. _____   10. _____

4. _____

Name _____ Date _____

Lesson 28
PRACTICE BOOK

Becoming Anything
He Wants to Be
Grammar: Commas in Sentences

Commas in a Series

- A **series** is a list of three or more words together in a sentence.
- Use a **comma** to separate the words in a series.

    It was <u>cold, wet, and windy</u> when he climbed the mountain.

Thinking Question
Are there three or more words listed together in the sentence?

Activity: Rewrite each sentence correctly. Add commas where they are needed.

1. He loved the wind the rocks and the outdoors.

    _____

    _____

2. He knew it would be windy snowy and cold on the mountain.

    _____

    _____

3. The climber made sure she had a coat gloves and boots.

    _____

    _____

4. I would rather read a book listen to music or take a nap.

    _____

    _____

5. He wanted to be a doctor a pilot or a teacher.

    _____

    _____

6. His parents friends and neighbors believed in him.

    _____

    _____

Introductory Words

- Use a **comma** after the introductory words *well*, *yes*, and *no*.
- Use a comma after order words such as *first*, *second*, *next*, and *finally*.
- Do not use a comma after *then*.

  Yes, I might want to try climbing one day.

Thinking Question
Is there an introductory or order word in the sentence?

Rewrite these sentences correctly. Add commas where they are needed.

1. First we looked up at the mountain.

   _____

2. Yes it was scary to think about climbing it.

   _____

3. No we were not about to give up.

   _____

4. Next we got all of our gear ready.

   _____

5. Then I started to get nervous.

   _____

6. Well I had only been climbing once.

   _____

7. Yes we started climbing as a group.

   _____

8. No we all stayed together as we climbed.

   _____

Commas in Sentences

**Read each pair of sentences. Fill in the circle next to the
sentence that uses correct punctuation.**

1. Ⓐ Climbers can be tall, short, young, or old.

   Ⓑ Climbers can be tall short, young or, old.

2. Ⓐ Yes, climbing is one of my hobbies.

   Ⓑ Yes climbing is one of my hobbies.

3. Ⓐ Well reaching, a goal takes lots of hard work.

   Ⓑ Well, reaching a goal takes lots of hard work.

4. Ⓐ She used paper, markers, and scissors to draw her plan.

   Ⓑ She used paper, markers, and scissors, to draw her plan.

5. Ⓐ First, you have to decide if you are willing to do the work.

   Ⓑ First you have to decide if you are willing to do the work.

Name _____ Date _____

Lesson 28
PRACTICE BOOK

Becoming Anything
He Wants to Be
Grammar: Spiral Review

Writing Abbreviations

- An **abbreviation** is a short way to write a word. Most abbreviations begin with a capital letter and end with a period.

Abbreviations	
Sunday	Sun.
Monday	Mon.
September	Sept.
any woman	Ms.
married woman	Mrs.
street	St.
avenue	Ave.

1–10 Write each abbreviation correctly.

1. October _____

2. avenue _____

3. Tuesday _____

4. doctor Smith _____

5. Thursday _____

6. mister Hill _____

7. December _____

8. April _____

9. mister Adams _____

10. street _____

Sentence Fluency: Combining Words to Form a Series

Choppy Sentences	Combined Nouns to Make a Series
He needs rope for climbing. He also needs gloves for climbing. He needs boots for climbing.	He needs rope, gloves, and boots for climbing.

Choppy Sentences	Combined Predicates to Make a Series
He wrestles. He scuba dives. He rides a bike.	He wrestles, scuba dives, and rides a bike.

Activity: Combine each group of sentences by forming a series of nouns, verbs, or phrases. Write the new sentence on the line. Add commas where necessary.

1. Erik climbs walls. He climbs mountains. He also climbs hills.

   _____

   _____

2. Jose wants to share his success with his parents. He wants to share it with his friends. He wants to share his success with his neighbors.

   _____

   _____

3. Maria never gave up. She never complained. She never made excuses.

   _____

   _____

4. Fong practiced in the morning. He practiced at night. He practiced on the weekend. _____

   _____

Focus Trait: Word Choice

**Read each step from instructions for starting a rock collection.
Rewrite the step with exact words and details to give more
information.**

1. Step: Get a box.

With Exact Words and Details:

_____

2. Step: Dig up some rocks.

With Exact Words and Details:

_____

_____

3. Step: Clean the rocks.

With Exact Words and Details:

_____

_____

4. Step: Put them away.

With Exact Words and Details:

_____

_____

5. Step: Read about the rocks.

With Exact Words and Details:

_____

_____

Words ending in **-er** or **-le**

Read the words in the box. Then choose the word that best matches each clue.

Word Bank				
apple	better	farmer	little	member
middle	rattle	struggle	summer	supper

1. a red fruit that is sweet to eat _____

2. someone who belongs to a group _____

3. a meal you eat late in the day _____

4. not big; small _____

5. a person who grows food crops _____

6. a toy that a baby shakes _____

7. in between the first and the last _____

8. the opposite of worse _____

9. the opposite of winter _____

10. a fight or argument _____

Words Ending with -*er* or -*le*

Basic: Write the Basic Word that answers each clue.

1. The goal of someone who is making funny faces at you is to make you do this. _____

2. If your aunt wants to marry, she will give you this. _____

3. Your goal is to make this color when you mix red and blue. _____

4. An archer's goal is to hit this part of a target. _____

5. A goal you plan to reach tomorrow is one you'll reach at this time. _____

6. Eating one of these a day can help you reach your goal of keeping the doctor away. _____

7. If a rooftop is your goal, this tool can help you. _____

8. Cooking a turkey dinner is the goal of many people in this month. _____

9. People often have a goal of building a snowman during this season. _____

10. A common goal during this season is to stay cool. _____

Challenge: Write two sentences telling how someone might reach a goal. Use both Challenge Words.

_____

_____

Spelling Words

Basic
1. apple
2. river
3. little
4. October
5. ladder
6. summer
7. purple
8. later
9. November
10. giggle
11. uncle
12. winter
13. center
14. double

Challenge
whistle
character

Word Sort

Write each Basic Word next to the correct heading.

Words that name seasons	
Words that name months of the year	
Words that name objects you can pick up	
Other words	

Challenge: Add the Challenge Words to your Word Sort.

Spelling Words

Basic
1. apple
2. river
3. little
4. October
5. ladder
6. summer
7. purple
8. later
9. November
10. giggle
11. uncle
12. winter
13. center
14. double

Challenge
whistle
character

Proofreading for Spelling

Find the misspelled words and circle them. Write them correctly on the lines below.

Spelling Words

1. apple
2. river
3. little
4. October
5. ladder
6. summer
7. purple
8. later
9. November
10. giggle
11. uncle
12. winter
13. center
14. double

Try Out for the Basketball Team

Welcome back to school! We hope your sumer vacation was super.

As you all know, winnter is the season for basketball. This year, tryouts for our team will be held the last Monday in Ocktober. Practices will begin early in Novembar. In January, we'll travel across the rivier to play our first game against the Dunkers.

We urge all interested students—new or old, big or littel—to try out for the basketball team. You won't have to make a basket from the senter of the court. You must, though, be willing to give dubble your all when it's needed.

So if you'd like to see yourself in our team's purpul uniform, just try out. That way, you won't be sorry laiter that you didn't.

1. _____   5. _____   8. _____
2. _____   6. _____   9. _____
3. _____   7. _____   10. _____
4. _____

Possessive Pronouns with Nouns

> **Thinking Question**
> *What pronoun shows ownership?*

- A noun that shows ownership is called a **possessive noun**.
- Some pronouns can take the place of possessive nouns.
- A pronoun that takes the place of a possessive noun and shows ownership is called a **possessive pronoun**.
- Some common possessive pronouns are *my*, *your*, *his*, *her*, *its*, *our*, and *their*.

POSSESSIVE NOUNS	POSSESSIVE PRONOUNS
<u>Carla's</u> uniform was dirty.	<u>Her</u> uniform was dirty.
Carla waited at the goal for <u>Manny's</u> pass.	Carla waited at the goal for <u>his</u> pass.

Activity: Write the possessive pronoun in each sentence.

1. When their team works well together, they almost always

   win. _____

2. Alex needs to practice his game. _____

3. Our coach has confidence in the team. _____

4. When will it be my turn to be goalie? _____

5. Don't forget to clean your uniform. _____

More Possessive Pronouns

• Some **possessive pronouns**, such as *mine*, *yours*, *his*, *hers*, *ours*, and *theirs*, can stand alone in a sentence, without a noun.

Our team can run faster than <u>yours</u>.

Thinking Question
What possessive pronoun shows ownership and stands alone in the sentence?

1–5. Write the possessive pronoun that stands alone.

1. My uniform is cleaner than yours. _____

2. Our team is much better than theirs. _____

3. This soccer ball is mine. _____

4. That family is hers. _____

5. The win is ours. _____

6–10. Rewrite these sentences using a possessive pronoun.

6. The soccer ball is <u>Carla's and her sister's</u>.

_____

7. Amy can stop any shot, but she thinks it will be hard to stop <u>Manny's</u>.

_____

_____

8. Everyone's uniforms are dirty, but <u>the one that belongs to you</u> is the dirtiest.

_____

_____

9. The uniform left behind was <u>Manny's</u>.

_____

_____

10. No one's family cheers louder than <u>my family</u>.

_____

_____

Name _____ Date _____

Possessive Pronouns

Read each sentence. Choose the best word in () to complete the sentence, and write the word on the line.

1. I showed the new student around (my, mine)

neighborhood. _____

2. These socks and shoes are (her, hers). _____

3. She may have scored the winning point, but the assist

was (my, mine). _____

4. I ran to (our, ours) bench. _____

5. The players understood the coach's words, but they

didn't know all of (her, hers) signals. _____

6. I found Jason's family, but I couldn't see where (mine, my)

family was sitting. _____

Kinds of Adverbs

- An **adverb** is a word that describes a verb.
- **Adverbs** can come before or after the verb they are describing.
- Adverbs tell *how, when,* and *where* an action happens.

Adverb That Tells How	Adverb That Tells When	Adverb That Tells Where
Manny **quickly** passed the ball.	We have to practice **often.**	We practice **here** at the park.

1–4. Write the adverb and what it tells about each underlined verb.

1. Gayle <u>cheered</u> loudly for Manny. _____

2. They <u>ran</u> away from the fire. _____

3. The game always <u>begins</u> at 4:00. _____

4. Our team <u>shook</u> hands happily with the other team.

_____

5–8. Rewrite the sentences below into one sentence.

5. The team played another game. They played the game later.

_____

_____

6. The goalie blocked the ball. He did it easily.

_____

7. We stop for water breaks. We stop often.

_____

8. Manny scores a goal. He always scores a goal.

_____

Sentence Fluency: Replace Repeated Possessive Nouns with Possessive Pronouns

Sentence with Repeated Possessive Noun	Sentence with Possessive Pronoun
Manny plays soccer because of <u>Manny's</u> family and <u>Manny's</u> interest in the game.	Manny plays soccer because of <u>his</u> family and <u>his</u> interest in the game

Rewrite each sentence. Replace the underlined words with the correct possessive pronouns.

1. Carla likes playing <u>Carla's</u> favorite sport.

   _____

2. If Hiro had it <u>Hiro's</u> way, he would try <u>Hiro's</u> luck at other sports like baseball.

   _____

   _____

3. <u>The uniform that is mine</u> was left at the field with <u>the shoes that are mine</u>.

   _____

   _____

4. Luisa had to go get <u>Luisa's</u> socks in <u>Luisa's</u> room because she forgot them.

   _____

   _____

5. At practice, Hiro's mom brings <u>Hiro's</u> dog, <u>Hiro's</u> sister, and <u>Hiro's</u> brother.

   _____

Focus Trait: Ideas

Read each pair of sentences. Underline the fact. Draw a line through the opinion. Then write a fact to replace the opinion.

1. In football, a touchdown scores 6 points. It is easy to score points.

Fact: _____

2. Golf is the hardest sport. Golfers use clubs to hit the ball.

Fact: _____

3. Swimmers should wear red suits. Many swimmers begin at a young age.

Fact: _____

4. A baseball catcher wears a mask. Everyone should have a turn to catch.

Fact: _____

5. All schools should have sports teams. Many children play sports.

Fact: _____

Name _____ Date _____

Lesson 30
PRACTICE BOOK

Sort the Words

Saving Buster
Phonics: Schwa Sound

Read each word in the box. Find the vowel that makes the schwa sound. Then write the word in the chart under the spelling of the schwa sound.

Word Bank					
about	actor	alive	cactus	camel	circus
engine	kennel	pencil	pilot	salad	wagon

schwa spelled *a*	schwa spelled *e*	schwa spelled *i*

schwa spelled *o*	schwa spelled *u*

Words that Begin with *a* or *be*

Basic: Write the Basic Word that completes each sentence.

Spelling Words

Basic
1. below
2. about
3. belong
4. around
5. again
6. alone
7. because
8. above
9. between
10. alive
11. behind
12. begin
13. along
14. before

Challenge
awhile
beyond

1. I was walking _____ my street when I spotted a kitten.

2. When it ran _____ my legs, I fell over!

3. Dad guessed the kitten is _____ two months old.

4. Dad said I could bring the kitten inside _____ it was cold out.

5. Then the kitten hid in a dark place _____ the couch.

6. _____ I could get it out, I had to move furniture.

7. The kitten jumped up on a shelf _____ the fireplace.

8. It followed a toy _____ in a circle.

9. The kitten made me laugh over and over _____ .

10. Dad and I agree that the kitten and I _____ together.

Challenge 11–12: Write a sentence about something you have seen an animal do. Use both Challenge Words.

_____

_____

Word Sort

Saving Buster
Spelling: Words that begin with
a or *be*

Write each Basic Word next to the correct heading.

Second syllable has three letters	
Second syllable has four letters	
Second syllable has five letters	

Spelling Words

Basic
1. below
2. about
3. belong
4. around
5. again
6. alone
7. because
8. above
9. between
10. alive
11. behind
12. begin
13. along
14. before

Challenge
awhile
beyond

Challenge: Add the Challenge Words to your Word Sort.

Proofreading for Spelling

Find the misspelled words and circle them. Write them correctly on the lines below.

Monday, July 9

    This past weekend, our family took part in a barn raising. I'd never heard abowt these events befoar. In a barn raising, a lot of people who bilong to a community get together to build a barn. No community member has to face the huge job of building a barn aloan.

    At first, I just walked arround the barnyard. I didn't know where to bigin to help. Soon, a man called from a beam abuve me. "Son, could you please bring me some nails?" he asked. I leaped into action becauze I wanted to be part of the group. I set up a ladder balow the man and handed him the nails.

    After that I worked hard all weekend, but that barn is done. It's a beauty! I would sure love to be part of a barn raising agenn.

Spelling Words

1. below
2. about
3. belong
4. around
5. again
6. alone
7. because
8. above
9. between
10. alive
11. behind
12. begin
13. along
14. before

1. _____   5. _____   8. _____

2. _____   6. _____   9. _____

3. _____   7. _____   10. _____

4. _____

Using *I* and *Me*

- Use the pronoun *I* only as the subject of a sentence. Always capitalize the word *I*.

    I am going to school.

- Use the pronoun *me* only as an object pronoun. When you talk about another person and yourself, it is polite to list yourself last.

    Julie handed the books to Lucy and **me**.

Thinking Question
Is the pronoun the subject or the object of the sentence?

Activity: Write the pronoun *I* or *me* to complete each sentence.

1. _____ watched my dog chase the ball.

2. Dad and _____ entered a dish in the potluck contest.

3. Amy went to the vet with my dog Sparky and _____.

4. My service dog helps _____ cross the street.

5. Can _____ help you plan the contest?

6. _____ liked the pasta salad the best.

7. The judge couldn't decide, so she gave the first prize
   to both Andy and _____.

8. _____ own a black dog named Ruby.

9. Ruby has been with my sister and _____ since I was
   five years old.

10. Someday _____ would like to train puppies to be
    service dogs.

Pronouns and Homophones

Homophones are words that sound alike but have different spellings and different meanings. Be sure to choose the correct homophone. Using the wrong homophone changes the meaning of the sentence.

Thinking Question
What are the clues in the sentence?

Homophone	Meaning	Example
its	belonging to it	The dog wagged **its** tail.
it's	it is	**It's** very cold outside.
your	belonging to you	I like **your** watch.
you're	you are	**You're** going to be late!
there	at or in that place	The book is over **there**.
their	belonging to them	**Their** dog can do tricks.
they're	they are	**They're** going to the store.

Activity: Read the sentences. Circle the correct homophones.

1. Dog training can be a fun activity for both you and **your you're** dog.

2. **Its It's** important to work with your dog every day.

3. Dogs perform best when **their they're** praised for good behavior.

4. If **your you're** patient with your dog, you can teach him or her to roll over.

5. **It's Its** important to train a puppy.

6. You can buy a leash at a pet supply store. Ask a clerk to help you when you get **there they're**.

7. The best time to train **your you're** dog is when he or she is young.

8. Dogs can still be trained when **there they're** older, too.

Correct Pronouns

Read each pair of sentences. Fill in the circle next to the sentence that uses the correct pronoun.

1. (A) Mom and I will make dinner.

   (B) Mom and me with make dinner.

2. (A) The dog brought the ball to Marisa and I.

   (B) The dog brought the ball to Marisa and me.

3. (A) They're dog was trained to be a service dog.

   (B) Their dog was trained to be a service dog.

4. (A) It's fun to teach a dog to do tricks.

   (B) Its fun to teach a dog to do tricks.

5. (A) I saw your mom at the store.

   (B) I saw you're mom at the store.

Making Comparisons

- **Adjectives** describe nouns. They can also show how people, places, and things are alike and different.

Comparing with Adjectives		
Compare Two	Add -*er*	taller
Compare Three or more	Add -*est*	tallest

- **Adverbs** describe verbs. For adverbs that end in –*ly,* add *more* to compare two actions. Add *most* to compare three or more actions.

1–4. Write the correct form of the adjective in parentheses to complete each sentence.

1. Molly was the _____ of all the service dogs. (small)

2. They were _____ than our other neighbors were. (friendly)

3. Of all of her classmates, Liz's voice is the _____. (strong)

4. Doug was the _____ member of the committee. (young)

5–6. Rewrite the sentences, combining each pair of sentences.

5. Ralph is smarter than the cat. He is quicker too. _____

_____

6. Of all the dogs in the park, Benny has the biggest feet.
He also has the longest tail. _____

_____

Conventions

Sentence with incorrect use of *I* and *me*	Corrected Sentence
Me and my mom did everything we could to help out.	<u>My mom and I</u> did everything we could to help out.

Sentence with incorrect homophone	Corrected Sentence
Their cooking wonderful food for the dinner tonight.	<u>They're</u> cooking wonderful food for the dinner tonight.

Proofread each sentence. Check for the correct use of the pronouns *I* and *me* and the correct use of homophones. Write the corrected sentence on the line.

1. David and me think the cooking contest will be fun.

_____

2. They gave they're food to me and my mom.

_____

3. The dog left the bone over their.

_____

4. Its amazing how much money was raised.

_____

5. Me and my friends think it's important to help you're neighbors.

_____

6. Its good when people help each other.

_____

7. You can help them by watching there dog.

_____

8. They're dog loves to play.

_____

Focus Trait: Organization

Read each paragraph. Cross out the detail that does not tell about the main idea. Then add a detail sentence that supports the main idea.

1. Other animals pull vehicles. Oxen pulled pioneers' wagons in the 1800s. Locomotive trains can pull many cars. Some kinds of horses pull sleighs and carriages.

   _____

   _____

2. Several types of animals carry people. For hundreds of years, people have ridden horses. Donkeys can carry people through rough terrain. Lots of kids ride bicycles to school. Some people also ride camels.

   _____

   _____

3. In a beehive, different bees have different jobs. The queen lays eggs. Worker bees do a few jobs. They help make wax. They also feed other bees and help protect the hive. Some people are allergic to bees.

   _____

   _____

4. Dogs do different kinds of work. Chihuahuas are a tiny kind of dog. There are herding dogs and police dogs. Some dogs are even actors!

   _____

   _____